D0200851

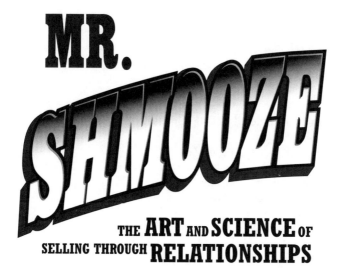

MR. SHMOOZE

THE ART AND SCIENCE OF SELLING THROUGH RELATIONSHIPS

Copyright 2002 Richard Abraham
Published by The Richard Abraham Company, LLC.
First Edition

Copyright © 2002 by Richard Abraham.
Printed in the United States. All rights reserved under the
Pan-American and International Copyright Conventions.

*This book may not be reproduced in whole or in part in any
form or by any means, electronic or mechanical, including
photocopying, recording, or by any information storage and
retrieval system now known or hereafter invented, without
written permission from the publisher.*

ISBN 0-9741996-0-5
SAN 255-5433

This book may be ordered from the publisher at
www.mrshmooze.com ,
or by calling 1-877-MRSHMOOZE.

The Richard Abraham Company, LLC
700 Commerce Drive, 5th Floor
Oak Brook, IL 60523
Phone: (630) 288-4759
Fax: (630) 288-4761
Email: rabraham@richardabrahamcompany.com

Contents

Prologue

We all know someone like Mr. Shmooze. He is the gregarious fellow at the office who makes everyone feel better by just showing up. She is the gal at the card party who tells the best stories with the juiciest, funniest anecdotes. They are the couple who we all want at our dinner parties because they electrify the atmosphere.

Mr. Shmooze can be a man or woman, young or old, tall or short, it really doesn't matter. Mr. Shmooze is not about surface appearances. Mr. Shmooze is about heart and soul, about good vibrations, and emotional connections.

I have spent twenty years studying the art and science of marketing and selling. There are many different theories, many techniques people use to present themselves and their goods and services in a positive light. And I have come to a very simple but powerful conclusion. There is not a selling system in the world that can match the exquisite elegance, the honesty and the raw power of a great relationship.

My Mr. Shmooze is a composite of characters from all walks of life whom I have had the privilege of engaging and observing. He is Drew, the commercial real estate broker in Chicago, who always seems to be the "lucky" winner of the big tenant transactions. It is Joan, perhaps the most important person I know, who has spent the past 10 years in the cancer ward of our local hospital. Her contribution goes far beyond nursing as she administers comfort and holds the hands of people as they face the ultimate challenge.

But the consummate inspiration for my story, the quintessential Mr. Shmooze, is my good friend Brett Hunsaker, a man based in Atlanta, but welcomed by people from New York to Los Angeles, from Chicago to Miami, who have come to know and love his unique approach to living.

Brett doesn't sell anything…he doesn't have to. Because if you mention his name to anyone who knows him, you will get a smile, a laugh and a warm response. The world has a way of rewarding such people handsomely, that is, people who give more than they take while they light up people's lives. This is a story about how one man does it and how we can all apply some of the magic of Mr. Shmooze to our work and lives.

Introduction

This is the story of a man who makes a phenomenal living by leading an extraordinary life. In fact, maybe I should reverse that sequence. This is the story of a man who leads an extraordinary life and happens to make a phenomenal living while he is at it.

You see, it is hard, perhaps impossible, to categorize a man like Mr. Shmooze because there is no one else quite like him. All I know is that if I have seen it once, I have seen it a hundred times…a person can be having a perfectly ordinary day when along comes Mr. Shmooze. Presto! A warm experience, a great memory, a special relationship, often for life. And once that special connection has been made, it is only a matter of time before mutual benefits are exchanged, often in the form of a business transaction.

Chapter One
BREAKFAST WITH MR. SHMOOZE

Like any good intern, I was determined to show up at our Atlanta office bright and early on my first day of work. I was quite pleased to find that I had arrived before Mr. Shmooze and was eager to see his surprised expression when he showed up. Suddenly my phone rang. I wondered who had my new number and who would be calling me at 7 a.m.

"Kid, I am pulling into the Ritz Carlton for breakfast. Just a minute…." Mr. Shmooze spoke to someone away from the phone. I would later come to know the man he was speaking to: Rudy, the carhop at the Ritz. "Hey, Rudy, how's your wife's cold? Better? Good. Listen, my client will be showing up in a silver Lexus. Would you have someone send it through a wash and have it parked in front when we come out? Thanks, buddy. Oh, here's a couple of those new Macanudos. Yeah, try these. They're great!" His voice became louder and I knew he was speaking to me again. "Kid, run over to a newsstand, pick up a new Forbes and bring it to the Ritz. My client's biggest customer is featured. Meet me in the dining room. Hey! Glad you're on board! We're going to have some fun!" As I hung up I could feel my adrenaline pumping. I was already in motion and, in just 60 seconds, had gotten a glimpse of the summer ahead: a summer with Mr. Shmooze.

1

Running toward the door, I happened to glance into Mr. Shmooze's office and noticed something peculiar. While everybody else's desks were covered with in and out boxes, neat and not-so-neat piles of important-looking documents and computers with impressive-looking screen savers, Mr. Shmooze's office was different. While by no means neat or organized, paper was replaced by books and magazines, boxes of cigars, pictures from golf outings and ball games. The pictures all had one thing in common: everyone was smiling, hugging and laughing!

I arrived at the Ritz around 7:45. As I pulled up, the attendant opened my door and said, "Hi, Robert! Mr. Shmooze is in the main dining room. Your car will be right over here when you come out!" I started walking toward the door and the attendant called back to me. "Hey, kid. You're working for a great guy! You're going to have a heck of a summer!"

The Ritz Carlton is the nucleus of business in Atlanta. It is elegant, sophisticated and it is the epicenter for business networking. As I worked my way through the bustling lobby and waiting area, I spotted the restaurant hostess standing in front of a magnificent, multilevel dining room. Before I could introduce myself, she looked at me and said, "You must be looking for Mr. Shmooze. Follow me." Before I knew it we were at his table, in the corner—and there he was—the one and only Mr. Shmooze, holding court.

Naturally, Mr. Shmooze was sitting in the most prominent position in the room, a place from which he could easily see everyone else coming and going and, of course, where everyone could see him. His client sat next to him but the table was large enough to seat several more people which, I was to find out later, often became the case. The table was full of various foods, juice, coffee and the morning news—*The Wall Street Journal*, *The New York Times* and *The Atlanta Constitution*. It was organized chaos. The energy was incredible.

"Here he is, Mr. Shmooze," announced the hostess, as I self-consciously approached the table. "Thank you," said Mr. Shmooze. "Did I say he was good-looking?" Both the hostess and I laughed and blushed. "You're going to be seeing a lot of him this summer, so take good care of him!"

"Kid, I want you to meet John Smith, VP of Marketing for U.S. Paper. John, this young man is studying at Georgia Tech and has the dubious distinction of being my intern this summer." I shook Mr. Smith's hand and took a seat, as Mr. Smith laughed heartily at my boss' self-deprecation and the vision of my summer ahead.

"Young man, I can guarantee that what you will learn this summer you would not learn at the Harvard Business School. You may not know it yet, but you just won the lottery!"

"Hey, speaking of the lottery, I've got six instant games here," Mr. Shmooze said. "C'mon, let's go through them. We'll split any winnings among the three of us!" Suddenly, we were scratching the cards with quarters, when I saw I had won $5.

"Hey, I won five bucks!"

"Me too," said Smith. He laughed and tossed it back to Mr. Shmooze. "Too bad I can't retire on this."

"I know—let's just leave them with the waiter."

"Great idea!" said Smith.

"Kid, sit down for a minute. Have you had breakfast?" I shook my head. Turning to the waiter, Mr. Shmooze called out. "George! Bring my friend a bowl of fruit and a croissant. Coffee?" he asked me, as he was already filling my cup.

"John, this young man is on a full basketball ride at Georgia Tech. Kid, John has two sons, aged 12 and 14, who are both playing ball in junior high. We were just discussing basketball camps. What do you think?"

"Well," I said, "I like Georgia Tech's camp because it really stresses fundamentals and teaches the kids about proper conditioning techniques. Lots of people do not understand how to relate weight training to basketball."

Mr. Shmooze seized the concept. "What a great point! You mean that, if John Jr. and young Jimmy learn some weight-lifting techniques, they will actually be able to jump higher?"

"You bet."

Mr. Smith was now leaning in and getting very excited. "Really? I thought jumping was something you were born with?"

"That's true," I said, "but we have guys who have increased their vertical jumps substantially through proper weight training."

Mr. Shmooze was now fully energized. "Wow, that's incredible! *Exactly how much* is 'substantial'?"

"Well, I know at least two guys who went from 26 inches to 32 inches."

"Thirty-two inches!" said Mr. Shmooze. "Holy cow! John, if John Jr. took his jumping to 32 inches, I bet he could dunk the basketball! Can you imagine Johnny cutting through the lane and doing a two-handed, reverse slam in the state tournament next year?"

"Yeah, baby!" yelled Mr. Smith as he reached out and high-fived Mr. Shmooze.

"Kid, take my cell phone, go out to the lobby and call the camp. Let us know what details you can find out before we leave." I left the table and was able to speak with a marketing person at Tech's basketball camp. She gave me dates and quotes and promised to send a brochure. When I returned, I noticed that two other people had joined the table.

"Kid, meet Joan Anderson and Helen Ralle. These are corporate services people from Premier Properties, a commercial real estate company. They 'happened' to be having breakfast so I asked them to join us for a cup of coffee."

Ms. Anderson was a no-nonsense type, and she came straight to the point. "So, Mr. Smith, your real estate is managed from your facilities-management group in Atlanta. Is that division run by Bob Nixon by any chance?"

"Yes, I know him, but not well."

Mr. Shmooze jumped in. "Hey, John, speaking of real estate, you probably know that Premier is one of the largest property managers in the country. They must buy more paper than anybody."

"You're right," said Smith. "We sell to a lot of the buildings, but I wish I could get to the very top of the big organizations so we could do some real pricing on scale."

"Joan, wouldn't that be Eric Taylor at Premier?" said Mr. Shmooze.

"Exactly."

"Man, this is perfect! Obviously Premier wants to handle U.S. Paper's real estate and U.S. Paper wants to sell Premier paper. I know Eric well—with everyone's permission, I'll set the whole thing up!" There were enthusiastic nods and smiles all around the table. "Wow, what a breakfast," continued Mr. Shmooze. "We're all going to make a *boatload* of money!" At that, everyone broke out into appreciative laughter, even the somewhat stoic Ms. Anderson. Then, when we were leaving, I watched in awe as Mr. Shmooze reached out and "touched" every player in this extraordinary production, again.

First, he signed the check and thanked our waiter, George, for his "usual outstanding service." Besides the tip, he also left the two winning lottery tickets for George. No cash changed hands.

Next, he stopped at the front desk, hugged the hostess and told her that when her father came to town the next week, he would be sure to have his good-looking intern drop off the two tickets to the baseball game he had promised. As we walked outside, Mr. Smith's car was clean and waiting, engine running, right in front of us. It occurred to me that George must have alerted Rudy we were coming.

"You really are too much!" said Mr. Smith to Mr. Shmooze as they hugged and slapped each other on the back.

"Knock 'em dead," said Mr. Shmooze. "I will fax you some information on basketball camps this afternoon."

Mr. Shmooze now turned to Rudy and handed him an envelope. "Rudy, here is a list of some people I will be meeting here for breakfast Wednesday."

"Okay, Mr. Shmooze! Hey, thanks for that article on night courses for real estate licenses you gave me last week. I think I am going to pursue that this fall, if I can figure out the details."

"That's great, Rudy! Robert, hop in the car with me. We'll pick up your car later!" With a surge of the engine and a slight peeling of the tires, we were off. Before I could say a word, Mr. Shmooze had his cell phone in hand and, in rapid fire, dictated points into his assistant's voicemail.

• "Mary, remember to get the two tickets for Susan, the hostess at the Ritz, to the Braves game next week. Besides the tickets, I want to send them two *nice* Braves hats. Also, her dad is a Glavin fan, so let's get an autographed ball as well.

• "I also want you to call the real estate license people and get a schedule and location of classes for this fall. Fax them to Rudy over at the Ritz Carlton this morning.

• "Call Jimmy Jeffries, my buddy who is the big donor at Georgia Tech. Tell him I would like to stop by and meet the head basketball coach for a minute this week, if possible, regarding his basketball camp.

• "Look up Commercial Property News on the Internet. Print out a copy of anything you can find on Premier's property management program. E-mail them to John Smith over at U.S. Paper.

• "Pull U.S. Paper's annual report and/or anything else you can find to locate their offices and plants around the world. Fax or e-mail them to Joan Anderson at Premier.

• "Check Amazon.com to see if you can find any books on weight training and basketball. I will call you back."

Mr. Shmooze hung up the phone and turned to look at me. I noticed how fast he switched focus. Suddenly I was the only person in the world.

"So, Robert, how are you doing? I can't tell you how glad I am you're here! I know Professor Mathis over at the school and you come highly recommended. He says you have enough energy for the job!"

"Well, I hope so, sir. I have a strong financial background and I'm certainly comfortable around the computer. I also—"

Mr. Shmooze gently, but firmly cut me off. "Hey, I know you're smart or Mathis wouldn't have sent you to me. And all that stuff is absolutely important, and will be for the rest of your career. But when I look for an intern, I also look for somebody who has it here—" Mr. Shmooze thumped his heart, "and here," he said, slapping his mid-section. "I want passion, guts, drive and enthusiasm. And I want someone who is in love with life, who loves people and who laughs hard and often. That's where I live." Mr. Shmooze's phone rang. "Excuse me," he said, clicking it on and taking the call.

"Shmooze here.... Billy! What's happening in the Big Apple this morning?... No way! Steinbrenner said that? The players must be really upset. Hey, I met with U.S. Paper this morning. Who is their lead investment bank up there?... Lehman Brothers? Know anybody there?... No, don't call him yet, but I may ask for an introduction the next time I'm in town. Anything I can do for you?... No problem. Hey, how did you like those new Macanudos?... Yeah, I agree.... Outstanding! I'll shoot you a box next week.... Over and out." Mr. Shmooze punched a button to hang up and then another to speed dial his phone.

"Mary, put Billy on the list for a box of Macanudos."

Now turning to me, Mr. Shmooze said, "Sorry, kid. Now, like I was saying, the name of the game with me is passion, heart, laughter. One of the things I do with my interns is stop occasionally and review. What have you learned so far this morning?"

"That you are a force of nature!" I said.

Laughing, Mr. Shmooze said, "Very good. Actually, you just illustrated one of my key points: Say something exciting, something positive, every single time you engage someone. *Every single time!* I like being called a force of nature! You just made me feel good. Made me smile. Made me laugh. Force of nature! And, guess what? I'll remember that."

I now began to recall the morning's events. "You called me, energized me, but also took a moment to welcome me. You also said we were going to have fun. I felt excited."

"Good!"

"When I got to the hotel, the car attendant was clearly waiting for me. I felt important."

"Uh-huh…."

"He—that is, Rudy—yelled to me that I was working for a great guy. He had caught your enthusiasm."

"Great! He's a super guy!"

"The hostess was also ready for me. She complimented me, too. You also made her—and me, come to think of it—feel good about you and about each other. You did the same thing with George, the waiter."

Mr. Shmooze smiled. "Professor Mathis was right about you, kid. Keep going!"

"When I sat down, rather than running through some stiff formalities, you went right to something Mr. Smith and I both have in common: basketball. Now that I think about it, you must have thought about that in advance." By now, Mr. Shmooze was grinning from ear to ear. "And when I told my story, you really drilled down on the details, in fact, the numbers. Why did you do that?"

"Very good. A keen observation. Most people speak in generalities. Numbers, if accurate, are not only more hard-hitting, but they are also ten times more memorable than words. Studies prove that. I guarantee that Smith will tell his sons *exactly* how much your buddies increased their vertical jumps through weights. From 26 to 32 inches, right?"

"Right."

"See what I mean?"

"Also, it is important, whether socializing or selling, to paint a *spectacular* picture for someone. To get the adrenaline flowing. To ignite their imaginations!"

"His son, slam-dunking in traffic?" I asked.

"Bingo! Let's not just talk about weight training and camps and basketball! Let's get excited! Let's get passionate! Let's dream together! What else did you learn?"

"I loved the way you ended the meeting. As they were leaving, you made each one of them feel special—again!"

"Always! Every time! These are my friends. This is my family, my team. We are on the planet together, right now, working, struggling, laughing, crying, every day. I love these people and I want them to know it. Every time!" Mr. Shmooze turned to me with a serious look, and continued. "Robert, if you remember nothing else from this morning's breakfast, remember this: Everyone makes decisions about who will be their friend, who will be their partner, who they will take a call from and, in business, who they will buy from based on two basic sensations: *pleasure and pain.* If they associate you with pleasure, you win! If they associate you with pain...." He shook his head. "Log these concepts, kid, because I am going to pound them home every day you are with me this summer."

"You know, Mr. Shmooze, in retrospect, it almost seems like you choreographed that whole breakfast."

"Right down to the carhop! Kid, it's amazing to me how many people *don't* plan their social events. They just throw people together and hope it works. I approach a social meeting like Lou Holtz approaches a football game. Like David Mamet approaches a play. Like Martha Graham approaches dance. This is my craft, my livelihood. I am out to make these encounters the best part of everyone's day. After all—my life depends on them! I don't mean to say you can't improvise, relax and have fun. The idea is not to be rigid and phony. On the contrary, everyone knows exactly what I am doing, and they love it because they see the passion and my honest efforts to make the meeting a success."

Mr. Shmooze suddenly veered off the freeway. The Indianapolis 500 came to mind. "Where to?" I asked. "Back to the office?" Mr. Shmooze froze for a moment, then his head jerked back and he laughed so hard, the windows rattled.

"Office?" he said. "Hey, kid," sweeping his arm 180 degrees around the ears, "*this* is my office." We pulled into Children's Hospital and he said, "Let's do something for the kids."

Chapter Two
TELLING A STORY WITH PASSION

I had never been to a children's hospital before, and upon entering I was struck by the cheerfulness and warmth of the main lobby. There were colorful, interactive exhibits everywhere and even a small McDonald's restaurant down the stairs. Of course, the idea was to take the fear out of a hospital visit and judging by the laughter and activity all around, the strategy was working.

Naturally, Mr. Shmooze seemed to know everyone in the hospital. The receptionist jumped up to give him a big hug. While others were busy signing in, Mr. Shmooze and I walked right into the inner core of the administrative area, winding up in a large meeting room where thirty or so people were awaiting our arrival. Again, many of them knew Mr. Shmooze, and there were hugs all around.

"Ladies and Gentlemen, let's bring this meeting to order," announced Dr. Ahern, the CEO of the hospital. "Many of you know Mr. Shmooze, but for those of you who have not met him, you're in for a real treat."

Dr. Ahern turned to Mr. Shmooze. "As you know, these are the folks responsible for much of our fundraising throughout the year. They are eager to learn your insight into selling, business development and relationship building. I have told everyone this will be approximately a two-hour session and that you have generously volunteered your time to conduct this seminar. Ladies and Gentlemen, our good friend, the legendary Mr. Shmooze!"

Mr. Shmooze strode to the front of the room, a huge smile on his face. He paced for a minute and scanned the room, seeming to make eye contact with each individual, many of whom smiled back.

"Folks, the reason I am obviously so happy to be here is because I am privileged to be among people who are literally doing God's work. So many talented people who could obviously make more money applying their skill and energy to selling real estate or trading stocks. But you folks are working for the *children* and it is an extraordinary privilege to be among you. In fact, I am the one who should be applauding you! Give yourselves a hand!" Mr. Shmooze leads them into an enthusiastic round of applause. I could feel the adrenaline rising in the room.

"Before I get started, I also want to introduce my new summer intern, Robert Richards. He is one of the brightest students at Georgia Tech and a basketball star to boot. Is this a strapping young lad, or what?" There was laughter and more applause from the audience, and from me, self-consciousness and that now-familiar adrenaline rush.

"Ladies and Gentlemen," Mr. Shmooze began, "today we are going to talk about two things that, when harnessed and executed in the context of sales, will increase your production dramatically. I am talking about 20 percent, 50 percent and more. I have seen it and I have the references to prove it.

"The beauty of these ideas is that they play right to your strengths and the strengths of your product." Mr. Shmooze walked toward a flip chart, then turned abruptly to the gathering. "By the way, somebody give me a quick description of what you are selling here." The people shifted a little bit in their seats, now knowing that the session was going to be interactive. People sat up a little straighter and everyone became alert. You could almost hear the adrenaline rising.

"Our product is the Children's Hospital," offered a lady in the front row.

"Good, thank you!" said Mr. Shmooze. "And what is your name?"

"My name is Jo Ann James." Mr. Shmooze walked over to Jo Ann and put his hand on her shoulder.

"Jo Ann, here is a Tootsie Roll Pop for being the first one to help me out this morning!" he declared, sparking a burst of energetic laughter from the crowd. "But let's drill down on that a little. Are you actually selling the facility? That is, the bricks and mortar?"

"Actually," a young man in the corner said, "our product is the medical services offered here. The finest services devoted to children in the country."

"Hear, hear!" seconded another young lady. People nodded with approval. Mr. Shmooze wrote "medical services" on the flip chart.

"That's great! I agree! This is one of the finest hospitals with the best services in the country. We are extraordinarily fortunate to have it in our community." He then wheeled to face the crowd. "By the way, is that a feature or a benefit?"

"Benefit!" someone yelled. The people, now feeling more confident, were getting into the flow. Mr. Shmooze kept going.

"Really. So if, God forbid, I have a sick child and I bring him to this beautiful facility and I have great doctors treating my child, I have experienced a benefit?"

"Absolutely," said a particularly emphatic lady named Phyllis. "That is exactly what I tell my prospective donors! Great hospital, great doctors, great service."

"Understood," said Mr. Shmooze. "Absolutely right. But let's stop and think about this for a second. These are all wonderful thoughts—but at this point in the process, have my child or I actually experienced a benefit?"

"Absolutely not," said Mark, jumping up, flush with revelation. All eyes turned to him. "You have not received a benefit unless we made you and your child feel better or cured your child altogether." Mr. Shmooze grinned, walked over to Mark and gave him a high five.

"Bull's-eye," he said. "Does everyone agree?" There was enthusiastic affirmation throughout the room.

"What about my Tootsie Roll?" yelled Mark in mock indignation. Mr. Shmooze wheeled around and threw one across the room, which Mark proudly caught with one hand.

"Seriously, I want to stop right here and let this monumental point sink in. Many, many products have wonderful features. Bigger, faster, cheaper! It is so tempting for us as salespeople to concentrate on them. But remember, the buyer cares only about the benefit to him, *personally*. Now, let's keep drilling down. We are not done yet." Mr. Shmooze turned to Mark and then to the group. "Mark, now that you have 'seen the light'— everybody say 'hallelujah!'— tell me what you would say to a potential donor now." The group was in a good mood now. Mr. Shmooze had them laughing, at ease, as Mark responded.

"Mr. Donor, we have a great hospital, wonderful doctors and extraordinary services. The bottom line is that we make children and their families feel better and are often able to cure their illnesses at Children's Hospital."

The room bubbled over with warm applause as Mr. Shmooze replied, "Mark, you are really getting in the groove. You have the beginning of a powerful benefit statement there. Let's break it down: You made four very important points: 1) It's a great hospital with 2) wonderful doctors offering 3) great service that 4) makes people feel better. Let's start with the hospital. Who says it's great?"

"We do!" shouted Mark, followed by cheers throughout the room.

"Of course, but the donor would expect you to say that. I bet your competitor says that." The room went quiet. "Who else thinks you're great?"

"The AMA!" a woman yelled. Mr. Shmooze turned towards her. "Really? What does the AMA say?"

"The AMA says we are one of the top three facilities in the country in terms of infrastructure and equipment."

"Now you're talking!" said Mr. Shmooze excitedly, recording the woman's points. "How about the doctors?"

"We have more pediatricians here than all but five other hospitals," offered a voice from the back of the room.

"Great—how many docs? Anybody know?"

"One hundred thirty," shouted someone from the other side.

"That's super! What else?"

"We are a top research hospital!"

"Says who?"

"Says *The Journal of Pediatric Medicine.*"

"Excellent! Great research. The *Journal* says so. Nice feature. What's the benefit?"

"Great research draws top talent, better doctors, better service."

"More good features. Any benefits?"

"More cures!"

Mr. Shmooze literally jumped at the audience. "Yes! Yes! And now for the coup de grace... how many more cures!? How much better service?"

The room, which had worked itself into a crescendo, went eerily silent. Finally, Mark said, "Mr. Shmooze, how could we find that out? How could we possibly be so precise?" Mr. Shmooze walked to the middle of the room.

"Ladies and Gentlemen, you have just reached the exact point that differentiates an average sales presentation from a great one and average productivity from awesome production. A buyer or, in this case, a donor, has the freedom to take his limited amount of money and choose to buy from an unlimited selection of goods and services. In this case, he has an even smaller allocation of money for what we'll call charitable purchases. The competition is absolutely fierce and the only way you are going to win is by accomplishing two things: First, establish an intimate, personal relationship with the buyer. I will come back to this in a minute. And second, be able to clearly and quickly explain how your product and services will benefit the buyer, *personally*, in memorably graphic and provable terms.

"For example, remember Mark's benefit statement and his four key points? Here is a way to prove those benefits and blow the competition out of their minds! Mark, come on up here." Mark stood and walked to the front of the room. "Listen to this," Mr. Shmooze said to the group before continuing with Mark. "Mark, I know you have many alternatives and many worthy causes to consider. I also know that a man like you wants your cause to apply your funds with the same intensity and discipline that you have used to create your wealth in the first place, right?" Mark nodded.

"An investment at Children's Hospital will make more children feel better and, in many cases, cure more of them than an investment in almost any other similar cause. The AMA rates us the number-one hospital in the region in terms of client satisfaction. We have 130 pediatricians on staff, 30 percent more than our nearest competitor. Due in large part to people like you, we are able to invest $30 million a year in research, providing a financial base that attracts top-notch talent. And, according to *The Journal of Pediatric Medicine*, we are able to produce more important ideas about children's medicine than any laboratory in the region."

Mr. Shmooze paused, scanning the room. Everyone was waiting for the knockout punch.

"Ladies and Gentlemen, we have now brought the buyer to the precipice, but it is going to take one more push for him to jump into our loving arms." Mr. Shmooze asked me to dim the lights a bit as Mark sat back down. "Everyone please close your eyes and take a deep breath. Relax a bit." Mr. Shmooze took an empty seat in the front row, then turned to the person on his left and said,

"Linda, what is your passion in life?" Somewhat startled, Linda tried to formulate a response. "Before you answer, please know that we are going to go around the room and get everyone's answer. Let's omit our work and our family. Think of something else—something you do somewhat selfishly. Something that turns you on!"

"I like to sing," said Linda.

"Really! Tell us about it."

"I sing in the choir at church on Sundays. Our choir has 30 members, and I am one of eight sopranos."

"Would you care to sing something to us now?"

"No!!" The room exploded with sympathetic laughter.

"Linda, what does it *feel* like when you and the choir are really on a roll? When the practice is paying off, when it is as good as it gets! Give us an example and really describe it for us!" As Linda sat up, an extraordinary transformation began to take place. Her eyes opened wide, her face became alert, excited. She began to use her hands to describe the experience of singing.

"Last Christmas Eve, we sang 'Oh Holy Night.' Everyone knows it is a challenging song and everyone waits for the high note toward the end. It either makes or breaks the experience. We struggled with it at rehearsal, but our choirmaster assured us that the inspiration and adrenaline of the live performance would inspire us to rise to the occasion. Well, the midnight mass came and it was a particularly beautiful evening. There was a gentle snow but it wasn't windy or harshly cold. The church was decorated beautifully and everyone was in a terrific mood. For the choir, the atmosphere was perfect—the congregation was joyfully singing along with every song. But then came our big number. Just before we sang it, our choirmaster gave us one last piece of advice: 'Folks, you sound terrific tonight,' he said. 'Now let's really go for it! Don't hold anything back. Give it everything you've got!'

"Mr. Shmooze," said Linda, "our voices had never sounded better. The harmonies were perfect and a funny thing happened—the better we sang, the stronger we became. When the big moment arrived, we literally exploded through the high note! I looked around the church and people were holding hands, crying, smiling—the emotions in the air were incredible. It was one of the most joyful moments of my life! To answer your question, I felt wonderful!"

Mr. Shmooze let the story sink in for a moment. The people in the room were completely transfixed. They were in church, with Linda.

"Linda, that was incredible. Thank you so much! Ladies and Gentlemen, you have just been privileged to experience a million-dollar lesson, in fact a priceless lesson, in the art and science of communication. What did Linda just teach us about the power of *passion* in communication?"

"Her whole body came alive," said John from the front of the room. "Her eyes lit up, her face became alive, her voice became stronger and more excited."

"I like the way she told the story," said Nancy, from the back corner. "I could picture the whole thing. I love midnight mass and 'Oh Holy Night' is my favorite song. I always wait for the high note!"

"Her passion came right through!" said Steve, a quiet fellow who had said little until now. "I know that feeling when I am playing tennis. Set point and you just rocket a passing shot right by your opponent. What a feeling!"

"That's it!" said Mr. Shmooze. "That is living! That is passion!" He was bringing the group alive. "Now", he continued, "let's take it back to our potential donor. Do you think he might react differently to our sales proposition if it were injected with the passion Linda applies to her singing and Steve draws upon when he's playing tennis?" A collective revelation filled the room as everyone matched their most passionate feelings with selling scenarios familiar to them. "Let's put it another way. Do you think that Pavarotti is passionate when he sings? How about Michael Jordan when he is taking it to the hoop?

"Ladies and Gentlemen, this is the great secret of all highly successful people in every walk of life. Franklin Roosevelt, Bill Gates, Einstein, John Lennon, Muhammad Ali—pick anyone who stands out—they all have one thing in common. They apply Linda's *passion* to their *work*, their *craft*. They do not reserve their passion just for 'personal' endeavors.

"Linda, *now* tell our prospective donor why, after all we have already told him, he should invest in Children's Hospital. Tell him the same way you just told us about your singing. Tell us about your *passion* for Children's Hospital!"

Linda jumped out of her seat and absolutely seized the moment. "Mr. Donor, here is the bottom line. Every day I see a new child— let's call her Marie, come into the hospital for the first time. They all have the same look. They are scared, worried and, in the child's case, often hurting. Marie has probably been to her own doctor a number of times and is naturally afraid. Afraid of probing, afraid of shots. She knows a trip to the doctor is often painful. But guess what! When she walks through the door at Children's Hospital, she sees a beautiful, fascinating, interactive mobile and immediately walks over to play with it. She then starts bantering with the other kids. She begins to laugh, relax—already she begins to feel a little better!

"On the way to her room, the hostess shows her the wonderful play area on her floor, the computer area, the internal TV station we have for the kids. Before long, one of our psychologists stops by and meets with Mom and Dad and offer ideas on how to keep Marie as upbeat and comfortable as possible. As time passes, Marie is treated by world-class physicians, she becomes involved with the other children, she is drawn into projects which keep her mind alert, positive and engaged.

"Mr. Donor, much of the time children like Marie leave the hospital cured and on their way back to health. Yes, some do not make it, but thanks to people like you, they actually find ways to enjoy their visit because it is as good as it can be... the best of its kind. Marie is given every possible chance, not only to be cured, but also to live, love and laugh as only a child can. There cannot possibly be a better cause for you to support in our great city!"

There was a long pause, as the intensity of Linda's pitch settled around the room. Then a tremendous ovation erupted from the group. Mr. Shmooze walked over and gave Linda a big hug.

"Folks, that is what communicating and—at the end of the day, selling—is all about. Let's recap. First, as we prepare our selling platform, we must be absolutely ferocious in converting *features* to *benefits*. We must take the *buyer's* perspective and remember to ask what is in it for him or her. Second, once we have made a commitment to our message, to our product, we must communicate with *passion*. Passion is contagious! It is uplifting! It will make our prospect feel better, more invigorated, more alive. He may not buy from us that day, but he will respect our passion and *he will never forget us*. That sets the stage for building a relationship, which we will talk about next time. Thank you!"

Mr. Shmooze basked in a huge ovation, then waded into the crowd. It seemed that each participant had been *personally* moved by his comments. I followed behind as instructed, quietly collecting business cards. I wrote anecdotes on the backs of them if people had spoken publicly or said something to Mr. Shmooze. Before the end of the day, Mr. Shmooze had dictated personal notes to each of them!

Then, in a flash, Mr. Shmooze and I were back in his car and, again, he was on the cell phone.

"Mary, good morning!... You already have a ball autographed by Glavin? How did you get it so fast?!... Of course. You're the best! A couple more items—I just finished at the Children's Hospital. I want to send a dozen tennis balls to a man named Steve. Tall guy, glasses. Our hostess, Joan Sherman, will know his last name. Also, one of the key participants is a singer. Check out Amazon and find her a nice book on choirs or singing.... Yeah.... Great! Talk to Robert for her name and info." Mr. Shmooze continued the give-and-take for several minutes before he signed off. I was amazed at how he touched so many people so fast and how he touched them in such special ways. *Ways they would never forget!*

It was nearing 12 noon and Mr. Shmooze was pulling into the parking lot at Blue Moon, a well-known local diner. Nothing fancy, but with a reputation for great burgers, steak and eggs, and the like. As we hopped out of the car, Mr. Shmooze said, "Kid, we're a little early—let's regroup for a second." We leaned against Mr. Shmooze's tan SUV and enjoyed the warm Atlanta sun. I had a thousand questions and hurriedly tried to organize and consolidate my thoughts.

"Mr. Shmooze," I queried, "you are moving so fast and covering so much ground that it is tough for me to get the essence of what you are trying to accomplish. Could you give me some insight as to what you are thinking as you go through your day?"

"Kid," said Mr. Shmooze, "like most things, my approach is simple to understand but, like everything else, it takes commitment to implement. Essentially, it is this: I consult for a living. I advise companies and other people how to increase their revenues. That means my product, to a great degree, is myself, my ideas, my connections. I believe most successful service providers succeed because of their ability to build relationships. That is what I teach and that is how I live. There is no way I could have any credibility whatsoever if I did not practice what I preach. I have, therefore, made it my top priority to build as many great relationships as I can."

"I understand that, Sir, but surely no one can have enough truly intimate relationships to depend upon them for one's living."

"Fair enough, but I am not trying to say that all relationships are created equal. What I am saying is that I want as many real relationships as I can get and that, whether the relationship is old or new, superficial or deep, my quest is to constantly find ways to keep it alive and make it better."

"The tennis balls."

"Exactly. Before today, I had never met Steve. But, he was kind enough to volunteer his thoughts at the seminar. He helped me. Most likely, he is more extroverted, more dynamic than the average guy. I have a simple choice. I can either let our interaction pass or I can begin to forge a bond with him by contacting him, showing my appreciation and, basically, making him feel good. Why not take advantage of that opportunity? One phone call to Mary and I have just opened the door to a whole new world – Steve's world.

"You see, Robert, I look at each and every person I meet as not just an individual, but as a huge, new network of lives, ideas, experiences. My job is not just to glaze over that network. My job is to plug in and get our networks communicating, interacting, succeeding together. I guess to you young techies, I'm like a walking, talking, human Internet."

Trying to look smart, I asked, "Well, Mr. Shmooze, exactly how many people do you think you are able to reach out and touch this way? Numbers are more impressive than concepts, you know."

Mr. Shmooze smiled and looked me straight in the eye. "After this morning, I'd say about half a million. Let's ask Mary later." Before I could close my gaping jaw, Mr. Shmooze was looking over my shoulder and shouting, "Hey, big dog! Over here!" A red Ferrari convertible slammed on its brakes, wheeled around the corner and pulled up next to us. Before the car had come to a stop, the passenger, an athletic-looking fellow had already stood up and drilled Mr. Shmooze right in the stomach with a perfectly spiraled football. Caught off guard, Shmooze dropped it and it went rolling under the other cars.

"Hey, Shmooze, nice hands! Don't let that ball get dirty. It's the one you asked for, autographed by Ditka!"

"You &#%$*@*!!" yelled back Mr. Shmooze. "That hurt! Kid,

grab the ball!" I was already searching between cars.

Lunch with Jimmy Page, the Ferrari owner, and Big John Wilson, former tackle for the Saints (and procurer of Ditka's autograph) went about the same as breakfast. Hostesses, waiters, stories, connections made, bonds hardened. And, most of all... laughter, adrenaline and good vibes. As we pulled out of the parking lot, Mr. Shmooze turned to me and said, "Quick, kid, hand me that Frisbee." I looked around and found a Frisbee that advertised a local cigar store. "Yeah, that's it. Give it to me."

Shmooze pulled up next to the open-topped Ferrari. As he started to turn out of the parking lot, he yelled at the former NFL lineman, "Yo, pretty boy!" and proceeded to whip the Frisbee to him at light speed. "Whack!" was the sound it made as the startled lineman promptly fumbled and dropped the disk. "Nice hands, meat head! No wonder the Saints cut you!"

We peeled out of the parking lot as hoots of derision and huge laughter—not to mention obscene hand gestures—receded in our rear-view mirror. "Get ready for the comeback tonight at Morton's," said Mr. Shmooze, laughing. "I'll probably get a forearm right in the face!" It was great fun, but my mind was already back to Mr. Shmooze's reference to "half a million" people before lunch.

"Mr. Shmooze, with all due respect, how do you figure you can have a relationship with half a million people?"

"Kid, I was just being dramatic to make a point. But listen up! You know all the advertisements you see for people like Merrill Lynch about 'the power of compound interest'? How savings builds upon itself and, over time, can blossom into truly incredible proportions? That is the way I feel about networking. Remember, each time you establish a relationship with someone, if it is a real relationship, you are plugging into his or her entire network as well. I have easily got a thousand names in my Rolodex of people I can call and engage. Each of those people has, say, 500 people of their own, assuming that they are only half as passionate about their product as I am. That is 500,000 people I can reach out and touch if I need to. And the number is compounding every day!"

Chapter Three
ELEVATION

Once the obligatory phone call to Mary was behind us, Mr. Shmooze proceeded to explain to me our next meeting.

"Kid, we are on our way to the Failsafe Security Company. Failsafe is one of the three largest commercial security firms in town and they are trying to increase their market share against a couple of national powerhouses. I am on retainer with them as marketing and new business development consultant." We soon found ourselves in a conference room with five Failsafe executives and salespeople.

"This week," Mr. Shmooze began, "I want to spend some time focusing on what I call 'elevating your game.' You have probably heard that expression before in a sports context: a professional athlete who suddenly emerges from the pack as a star, winning a streak of golf tournaments, or raising his scoring average to the top of the NBA. If you break down what is happening in these cases, inevitably the person is doing many things well. In fact, as success breeds confidence, every part of the athlete's game—driving, chipping, putting—improves simultaneously. The athlete *elevates*, mentally and physically, to the next level. But it all starts with the little things.

"This phenomenon happens in sales as well. What I want to talk about today is how each and every part of relationship building and selling can be improved and 'elevated,' time after time, eventually elevating your entire game, lifting you to the next level of productivity and success! Let's get started. David, what is the profit margin of your business?"

"Around five percent," said the executive sitting at the head of the table.

"Obviously, five percent is fiercely competitive," responded Mr. Shmooze. "Would you say that your basic service is, therefore, considered somewhat of a commodity by your clients and customers?"

"Unfortunately, yes", David said. "There's really no more room for price reduction. We and our competitors all charge almost the same price for security service."

"How does your service compare?"

"We like to think we are the best. Honestly, we are certainly better than most. We get good grades from our customer service surveys."

"Okay. I am not here to analyze your core customer service today, so I am going to assume, for the purposes of this discussion, that it is competitive. And I will assume it is not cost-effective to make your *core* service a differentiating factor in this context. The bad news, of course, is that, since you are trying to make your living selling a commodity, by definition, it is nearly impossible to differentiate one commodity from another at the core level. But here is the good news—in fact, the *great* news! In a commodity environment, it all comes down to differentiating yourself as a human being. The best salesman with the best relationships wins. It all boils down to you! And how do you differentiate yourself? By elevating your game. And I'm going to show you how!

"For the next hour, we are going to literally go crazy! I want crazy, absurd, wild ideas. The more outrageous the better. There are no bad ideas. No criticism. You are going to be amazed what happens to your brains when we open them up and let the electrons really fly!" Mr. Shmooze turns to a salesman. "Jim, name a customer for me."

"Dan Gooding, VP of Facilities Management for Coca Cola." Mr. Shmooze stands and moves to the flip chart behind him.

"He is your buyer at Coke?"

"Yes."

"Profile him! Looks, size, style, etc."

"Dan is around 5-foot-10 inches tall, 170 pounds, good shape. Sharp dresser, even when casual."

"What does his office look like?"

"Nice office, well-organized."

"Clean desk?"

"Come to think of it, yes."

"Pictures?"

"Yes—a lot of them. Family and business pictures."

"What kind of business pictures? With important people? Dinners?"

"Both. Also golf outings."

"So, he is sociable and socially conscious. Probably status conscious."

"Yes, I'd say so."

"What is his passion in life?"

"I'm not sure. His family, maybe?"

"Okay. Let's play Sherlock Holmes. Does he ever talk about his kids?"

"You know, his one boy is quite a golfer. I think he is around an eight handicap or so."

"How old?"

"I think a freshman in high school—but he's playing for the varsity."

"Does his dad go to his golf meets?"

"As often as he can."

"BINGO!!"

"Folks, we have just been handed the keys to building an intimate relationship with this buyer. The pictures in his office show that golf is important to him. He is probably pretty good in his own right but was not good enough to be a professional. Now it's his son's turn. What can we do for this fellow?"

"Invite him to play golf!" offered Ted from the corner seat.

"Invite whom?" asked Mr. Shmooze.

"Dan, the buyer."

"Anybody else?"

The executives looked around the table at each other, searching for the answer. Finally, one of them, Andy, suggested, "Another Coke guy?"

"Keep talking."

"Dan's son!" shouted Ted, the light bulb going off in his head.

"Right on," said Mr. Shmooze, writing it down. "Ted, you just *elevated!* Everybody invites Dan to play. I'll bet no one invites his son. Who else?"

"Someone who can do him some good career-wise?" asked David.

"Another good idea. Remember, though, we are focusing on his *passion.* His passion is his son and, especially, his son's golfing."

"How about a friend of his son? Someone else from the golf team?" Jim said.

"I love it! Elevation!"

"For now, let's assume it is his son's friend—by the way, what is Dan's son's name?"

Jim said, "I'm not sure."

Mr. Shmooze wheeled around and threw a crushed paper cup at Jim. Jim was then immediately pelted from all sides, as the room filled with laughter. "Let's call him Bill. Assume we have now invited Dan, Bill and Bill's friend, Bob, to play, and they have accepted. Where should we play?"

"Forest Glen!" said Ted.

"Sleepy Hollow!" Andy shouted.

"Hey, have you played Cog Hill?" asked John. "It's off the charts."

"Great choices. But what do you say we ask…" Mr. Shmooze paused in mid-sentence, waiting. The room responded exuberantly, in unison.

"BILL!!"

"You bet. Let's tell Dan that we will take him and Bill anywhere in the area. It's up to Billy. He spends days with Dan, researching clubs, building excitement. They choose Cog Hill. Now what?"

"We set up lunch, the game and dinner later." Ted offered.

"Okay, the classic program. Remember, we are focusing on Bill. How do we knock his socks off? How do we make this the most *memorable* golf outing of this young man's short life? How do we elevate the experience?!"

"Fly in Tiger Woods," David laughed.

"Yeah, right!" countered Andy.

Mr. Shmooze jumped in. "Not so fast! We want to get crazy, right? Let's follow that track for a minute. Who's the pro down there?"

"Sam Berger," said John.

"Sam Berger—he's a well-known teacher, isn't he? Authored a couple of instruction books?" Several heads around the table nod in agreement. "How about a note from Sam welcoming the boys, in advance, along with an autographed book?" Murmurs of enthusiasm and excitement floated around the room. "C'mon, keep it going. How do we get these kids really psyched up?"

"How about a complete care package, sent to their house in advance?" said Jim.

"I like it! Keep going! Elevate the care package!"

"How about a golf shirt," continued Jim, "and maybe a sleeve of balls and tees."

"Great. Elevate the shirts!" Ideas now began to come from all sides at machine gun rates. It was adrenaline time!

"Club logo!"

"Bobby Jones!"

"Nike!"

"Jack Nicklaus!"

"Good, all good—but really elevate now, make it special."

"How about *their* names embroidered on the sleeves?" said David.

"There it is! Elevate the golf balls!"

"Same thing," added Ted. "Personal names!"

"Great! The care package now has a personalized shirt, personalized balls, autographed book, and a note from the pro," said Mr. Shmooze. "Anything else?"

"Yes," offered Jim. "These kids are good. Let's send them cards with the course layouts, pin placements and yardage in advance. They will start playing the course in their heads."

"Perfect! Now, let's elevate the day. Dan and the kids have now received the care package and have been talking about the game for weeks. How are we going to make the day sensational? Picture the sequencing in your minds. What happens first?"

"They pull up to the caddy area and drop off their clubs..." Andy began.

"Good—let's elevate that experience. Let's make sure the greeter calls the boys by name and tells them he hears they are outstanding young golfers!" The group loved it! High fives went around the room—with Mr. Shmooze, with me, everyone! "Wait" interrupted Mr. Shmooze. "We're not done! What else?"

"Let's have the caddy master put new towels with the company logo in their bags," John said.

"Let's make sure their caddies are a little younger than they are so they can show off!" Ted added.

"Love it! What's the next sequence?"

"Locker room!" Andy and Ted shouted at once.

"Right. Elevate the locker room sequence."

"The locker room guys are usually pretty good," said David. "Guest lockers, names on the locker, shoe shine."

"Elevate!"

"How about a personalized Dopp Kit?" wondered Andy.

"Good one! What's next?"

"Lunch in the men's grill," suggested Jim.

"Elevate lunch."

"Let's have the pro stop by and chat with the boys!" Ted exclaimed.

"Hey, why stop there?" said Andy. "How about a quick group lesson at the driving range?"

"Now you're talking! The pro stops by at lunch and offers to give a chipping lesson before tee time. Beautiful! Let's turn to the match: Elevate!"

"Well, if this were some sort of corporate event, there would be various contests," said Jim. "You know, closest to the pin, longest drive. But I'm not so sure about those ideas with just a foursome."

"Wait, I think you're on to something," said Mr. Shmooze. "Could you get the pro or one of his assistants to play a couple holes and have a 'beat the pro' contest? You know, he tees off first, then anyone who gets closer to the hole or out-drives him gets, say, a sleeve of balls."

"Sure, I think they would do that," said David. "They will often play an entire hole with you."

Ted was really into it. "Anyone who beats or ties him could win a prize!" he said.

"Excellent! Anything else?"

Andy almost jumped out of his seat. "I got it! A videotape of everyone's swing!"

"I love that idea. You know why? Because you could send the videotapes to everyone a week or two later, refreshing the whole event. All right, great job! This is what great performers do when they *elevate* their games. This is what great salespeople do when they build relationships through special events. To sum up and drive the point home, I like to paint a picture of the difference between the lazy salesperson, who I will call Mr. Mope, and the super salesperson, who I call—"

"Mr. Shmooze!" came the unison response. Mr. Shmooze smiled and gave the team a double thumbs-up, as he wrapped up the meeting.

"Mr. Mope notices his client likes golf. Mr. Shmooze notices his client's *son* likes golf. Mr. Mope invites his client to play golf. Mr. Shmooze invites his client, his client's son *and* his son's buddy to play golf. Mr. Mope makes the reservations and waits for the big day. Mr. Shmooze calls the pro, gets autographed books and organizes a kick-ass care package to pump up excitement *before the event!*"

Mr. Mope buys shirts and balls. Mr. Shmooze buys *personalized* shirts and balls. Mr. Mope alerts the caddy master to take the clubs and assign caddies. Mr. Shmooze arranges for the caddy master to fuss over the boys, call them by name, reserve special caddies and place new towels in their bags. Mr. Mope's locker room attendant meets the guests in the locker room, assigns guest lockers and shines shoes. Mr. Shmooze's locker room attendant caters to the boys, has *their* names on the lockers and hands them a special Dopp Kit when they arrive.

"Mr. Mope arranges for a nice lunch, warm-up at the driving range and the usual, 18-hole round. Mr. Shmooze arranges for the pro to drop by at lunch and give a group chipping lesson before tee-off. Mr. Shmooze also arranges for several surprises and contests with the pro during the round. Mr. Mope signs off after the day. Mr. Shmooze sends a videotape to his guests a week later. He also arranges for his assistant to monitor Bill's golf meet results so he can leave congratulatory messages for Dad throughout the season.

"Finally, let's go back to the beginning. What did we miss? Think of his office."

"A picture!"

"You bet. The client, the boys and *Mr. Shmooze*! Forever! Now, Gentlemen—assuming Mr. Mope and Mr. Shmooze are selling competitive commodity services, who do you think has the best chance of building a relationship with Dan from Coke over the long haul? On three—one, two, three—"

"Mr. Shmooze!"

"I can't hear you!"

"MR. SHMOOZE!!"

"Right on, my brothers! And remember… elevate, elevate, ELE-VATE! Everything, every person, every time. You will become successful beyond your elevated dreams!"

"C'mon, kid," said Mr. Shmooze, turning to me. "I just led these thoroughbreds to the water. They have some drinking to do. Good luck, boys! See you in two weeks!"

Back in the car, Mr. Shmooze called Mary, leaving her a message to send boxes of personalized golf balls to the Failsafe guys. "I want the word 'Elevate' printed on each one," he said. Then he paused a moment. "What did you think, kid?" he asked me.

"I guess we all want to elevate, and we all think we are elevating. It is quite an eye-opener to watch you orchestrate true elevation."

"Kid," said Mr. Shmooze, turning into the Ritz Carlton again to get my car, "the key to elevation is *focus*. Artists and architects and other creative people notice everything they see—colors, textures, subtle combinations. They are masters of observing details and, as a result, are able to create some of the most beautiful things in our culture. But beauty can also be created in the abstract sense, through a process or, in a salesman's case, in the art of selling and relationship building. But the devil is absolutely in the details. And when we break things down, each and every single component can be made a little bit better—eventually elevating the whole message in the process.

"A picture is worth a thousand words, huh kid? I will pick you up tonight at 5:30. Then you'll *really* see some elevation!"

Chapter Four
DINNER A LA SHMOOZE

M r. Shmooze picked me up in front of our office at 5:30 sharp. We were on our way to Morton's, a classic steakhouse and one of several places where Mr. Shmooze had long established himself as the unofficial "mayor." When he pulled up, Mr. Shmooze, as usual, was on the phone—this time with the head maître d' at Morton's, attending to a dizzying variety of small details. He hung up and picked up right where we had left off earlier in the day.

"Client events are really at the heart of everything I do," Mr. Shmooze told me. "My overall goal is simple: I want everyone who attends to not only have a great time, but also to tell everyone else they had a great time. I want everyone to hope they get invited to the next party." He stopped and put the car in park, with the engine running. "Now, there are two keys to the success of any event: One, you need to break the event down to its component parts and make sure *each* part exceeds everyone's expectations."

"Elevation," I said.

"Bingo," said Shmooze.

"Two, you have to be an active director, like a movie director, choreographing the event and *watching everyone* like a hawk. It's okay to participate and have fun, but make no mistake about it— you are *working* the entire night.

"Take the dinner we will be having tonight. Keep an eye on the following components and tell me later what you have observed. Tell me whether you would grade each part 'average' or 'meets expectations' or 'excellent'—that is, 'exceeds expectations.' Take some notes discreetly. I will be interested in your observations. Here are the key components: car valet, hostess, bartender, dinner waiter, wine, appetizers, main course, dinner conversation, dessert, gifts and after-dinner drinks." I was writing as fast as I could when, suddenly, my door was opened by the Morton's car valet.

"Welcome to Morton's, sir... yo! Mr. Shmooze!"

"Kid, meet Bobby, the best car man in town. Bobby, this is my summer intern, Robert. He plays at Georgia Tech and he can hit the trey!"

"They can use it," said Bobby. "The ACC is going to be brutal this year."

"Bobby, let's review your plan," said Mr. Shmooze. "What have you got for me, baby?" Two young men walked up as Bobby began to speak.

"Mr. Shmooze, we are prepared for seven cars tonight. I have your list of names and cars and I will greet everyone by name. My partners here will detail all seven cars. We have the car wash stuff out back. Julie will alert us when the folks are finished with dinner so we will be waiting for them."

"Julie's the hostess," Mr. Shmooze said to me. "Yes, go on," he added.

"We will accept no tips. I will simply tell everyone it's taken care of. Absolutely no exceptions. We will attach the key rings you gave me to each set of keys. We will also place the cassettes or CDs you gave us right under the radio, in the ashtray, with your note. If anybody has had too much to drink, we will have a limo on standby who we can radio upon your request."

"Kid, what did I tell you? Is he the best or what?" Mr. Shmooze stretched out his arm between the three men and instructed everyone, including me, to touch fists. Then, like a quarterback breaking a huddle, he took both sides of all the hands, shook them and shouted, "Ready... for... showtime!" We whooped and screamed, with high fives all around. The car team was ready!

As we rolled in the door, we were met by Julie, the maître 'd named Ron and the associated staff. Everyone hugged. Then, for a moment, Mr. Shmooze huddled with Julie.

"Mr. Shmooze, I have your list. Everyone will be greeted by name. I will gather coats and I will hold the coat checks myself. I've memorized these anecdotes you suggested I use for each person," she went on, hesitating as she added, "only I am a little concerned about the football player I am supposed to tell, 'I hear you have great hands.'" She chuckled, and laughter broke the tension all around. "I will bring each person to you in the bar and tell Fred, the bartender, who is arriving so he can react accordingly."

"Thank you, Julie," said Mr. Shmooze. "Oh, you mentioned last week you like Lancôme products. Here is a little something my wife recommended." Mr. Shmooze handed her a gift box with a Lancôme moisturizer product inside. There was a second hug, with smiles all around.

We made our way into the lounge, where Fred, the bartender, was waiting for us. Our drinks were waiting on the bar. Mine was a sparkling water. "When you are hosting," said Mr. Shmooze, nodding toward the drinks, "start slow and build up steam. Remember, we are working!"

"How do you see things shaping up tonight?" asked Fred.

"This is a fun crowd, but I want to keep things under control, at least until after dinner. Let's figure one drink in the lounge, then we'll go to wine at the tables. Some of us will probably be back later to let our hair down." Fred glanced quickly at Mr. Shmooze's balding head but, before he could say anything, Mr. Shmooze quickly preempted him. "Don't even go there!" They both had a good laugh.

"Okay, I have my list of names, drinks and anecdotes," said Fred. "How does this gal, Denise, have time to be a top investment banker, a mom and teach a class at an inner-city high school?"

"Good question," answered Mr. Shmooze. "Ask her." Suddenly, Mr. Shmooze was lofted airborne, upwards from behind, firmly in the grasp of a powerful bear hug. He was being shaken up and down—no mean feat, considering his own 250-pound frame.

"Wise guy, huh?!" bellowed Big John, who had snuck up behind Mr. Shmooze and signaled Fred not to give him away. "I'll show you good hands, you turkey!"

Fred held out a Grey Goose martini to Big John and said, "All right guys! There will be no broken ribs in my bar tonight." The floor shook as Big John dropped Mr. Shmooze to grab the martini.

"Jeez," said Mr. Shmooze, "at least grab me after I have taken a breath. I almost blacked out, you animal!" The two of them continued their playful ribbing. Meanwhile, John's partner was flirting with the hostess at the bar entrance. Fred quietly mixed him a Bacardi and Coke and walked around the bar to deliver it to him. Page, not a regular at Morton's, looked at the drink, then at Fred, then just shook his head with a laugh.

"Shmooze," he called out, "you're the man!"

The ritual was repeated as the rest of the dinner guests arrived. Mr. Shmooze had made arrangements for eight guests, plus the two of us. There were four women and six men from various walks of life. I soon discovered, however, that they all would have something in common.

Dinner, of course, was outstanding. The wine captain did not just serve wines: He brought out several wonderful red and white wines, taking time to explain where they were from and why they were ready to drink at that moment.

Appetizers were served right away. But not just *any* appetizers— two gigantic, spectacular plates with a variety of seafood were placed at each end of the table. The food was shared "family style," an experience that further bonded the guests, as they "oohed" and "ahhed" over the selections, exchanging compliments.

We never saw a menu. When it came time to order, the waiter simply announced that Mr. Shmooze had chosen three entrées for the group—one meat, one fish and one pasta—each of which the waiter described in great detail. Rather than going through the usually laborious and time-consuming ritual of choosing from a menu, the selections took only about two minutes total, thus preserving the pace and momentum Mr. Shmooze had carefully orchestrated.

Mr. Shmooze then did something I had never seen before. He stood up and announced, "I want Jim, Bill, Larry and Steve, and myself, to move two places to the right." After some good-natured grumbling, the four of them got up and joined Mr. Shmooze in changing seats. The staff, whom Mr. Shmooze naturally had alerted, quickly swooped in to remove plates and replace silverware.

Within moments it became clear what a terrific concept this was. Everyone immediately engaged a new set of people and the simple act of moving sent a fresh charge of adrenaline through the atmosphere. The move was repeated again later, prior to dessert. But Mr. Shmooze had other tricks to pull from his sleeves. For example, about halfway through the entrée, he stood up and announced it was time to play a game. He passed out cards and pens to everyone, telling them to "Write down one thing about yourself that is interesting or unusual or that you think people might be surprised you have done." He said he would then collect the cards and guests would try to guess who matched what experience or characteristic. Of course, this sent yet another adrenaline rush through the group as everyone immediately became pleasantly self-conscious. The atmosphere crackled and the volume rose as questions and wisecracks flew in all directions: "Is this going to go beyond this room?" "Should we stay away from our sex lives?" "Are there any reporters in the room?"

Needless to say, the next half-hour was filled with wonderful karma as people shared an incredible variety of their interests and experiences. The buttoned-down lady with Goldman Sachs had once sung in a punk rock band in college. Our NFL lineman was a gourmet cook whose specialty was soufflé. Jim Page and his daughter worked in a soup kitchen every Sunday morning. Nancy, the sales rep for a lighting company, raised and trained purebred standard poodles. By the time we had finished the entrée, virtually all walls between people had been broken down. Everyone now had something in common with someone else at the table. The body language was wonderful as people leaned in to learn more about each other's fascinating lives. Meanwhile, Mr. Shmooze had picked up another round of passionate insight. I was already envisaging Mary on the Internet looking up books on dogs and recipes for soufflés.

At the appropriate time, Mr. Shmooze rose again and announced that dessert and cordials would be served in the lounge. Soon, everyone was back with Fred, as he stood over a variety of desserts at the bar. Each person chose a sampling of the offering, which were portioned and distributed by a waitress. Later, I asked Mr. Shmooze why he did this.

"The problem with dinners is that they can run too long. People can get tired after the main course, and that means losing a lot of momentum. I like to get people up and moving around, and people who need to leave a little early have a chance to scoot out."

Of course, a dinner with Mr. Shmooze had to include a coup d'état. Sure enough, along came Jerry Gleade, Morton's General Manager.

"Folks, it was a pleasure serving you this evening. We certainly hope to see much more of you in the future. Please accept this token of our appreciation." Jerry proceeded to pass out nicely wrapped boxes, which, I later learned, were a set of fine Morton's steak knives. This, of course, had been arranged in advance with Mr. Shmooze. It was a classic win/win situation for Morton's and for the new customers Mr. Shmooze had brought to the establishment.

As our guests began to make their exits, a wonderfully strange thing occurred. People who barely knew each other when the evening started were hugging, backslapping and expressing the warmest possible feelings. And, of course, there was much laughter and head shaking when their sparkling clean cars rolled up!

Finally, it was down to just Mr. Shmooze, Page, Wilson and me at the bar. I watched as the three of them played liar's poker. There was a warm glow as the colorful cast of characters from Morton's gathered for a recap to go with their nightcap.

"Guys," said Mr. Shmooze, "what do you think of my team?"

They both had a lot to say: "Unbelievable." "The best!" "You folks are too much!" As the praises continued, the Morton's crew basked in the warm glow that is "Mr. Shmooze."

Chapter Five

ENTREPRENEURS: A SPECIAL BREED WITH SPECIAL NEEDS

Several days later, I picked up Mr. Shmooze at the airport. We had an 11 a.m. appointment with a wealthy and successful owner of a commercial cleaning business.

"Hey kid, how are you doing? Meet Jim Keck. He and I sat next to each other on the plane and I told him we could drop him off on the way to our appointment." Naturally, Mr. Shmooze had engaged the man next to him on his trip back from Chicago. As they talked while we drove downtown, Mr. Shmooze explained to me that the man was the CFO of a midsized trucking company, had two adopted daughters ages five and eight, was an avid fly-fisherman and had just purchased a new home in Buckhead. After Mr. Shmooze got off the phone with Mary (he asked her to purchase a book on fishing in Georgia and a Buckhead restaurant guide for the CFO), we turned our attention to the next meeting.

"Okay kid, let's focus. The guy we are going to meet started and runs the most successful commercial cleaning company in town. He is a great salesman, a sharp operator and is absolutely ferocious about customer service."

"No wonder he is doing so well," I added. "What's not to like?"

"Exactly, but he has a problem. You see, he is trying to expand geographically, but entrepreneurs often get trapped by laying their own standards of passion and intensity on their employees. The pressure causes good people to go elsewhere. This fellow is caught in exactly such a conundrum."

"Is that what you're going to tell him?" I asked.

"Nooooo, no way! You do not *tell* a successful entrepreneur anything. Strong entrepreneurs, by nature, are successful because they have supreme confidence in their own ideas. They have to be optimists to survive and they are tough as nails. In short, since they already think they know everything about every subject, they do most of the talking. No, the key to this meeting is twofold: One, we will shut up and listen. Two, when Irving sees the light, believe me, it will be *his* idea."

When we arrived, Irving's secretary, Colleen, showed us to his office in the corner of the building. It was evident who was the boss of this operation. Plaques and awards were everywhere, as well as pictures of Irving with everyone from George Bush to Jack Welch. As we came around the corner, there was Irving, in front of his office. But instead of standing, he was crouched down in a three-point stance, as if he was set on the line of scrimmage.

"C'mon, Shmooze," he said, "Let's see what you've got!" Shmooze hunkered down, then bolted off the line. When the two of them collided, the earth shook.

"Are you guys ever going to grow up?" mocked Colleen as she rolled her eyes.

"Shmooze, you're getting soft!" yelled Irving, rubbing his forearm.

"I don't like to pick on old guys," countered Shmooze, limping into Irving's office on his now aching left knee.

"C'mon, kid, how about you?" asked Irving.

"Wrong game," I parried, "but any time you want to play h-o-r-s-e, I'm in."

"I can beat you at that, too," challenged the indefatigable entrepreneur. Once we settled down, it took Irving all of 30 seconds to jump-start the meeting.

"Shmooze, you know the drill. I have built this business from scratch and we are now doing around $50 million in sales. We are number one in this market and we provide the best quality and service in the industry. But I can't grow much more here, so I recently opened offices in Charlotte and New Orleans. They have been open for a little over a year now, but I can't seem to get over the hump with them."

"Who is marketing or selling for you in those markets?" asked Mr. Shmooze.

"I had headhunters recruit some of the best people around. Real thoroughbreds—at least on paper."

"Are revenues growing?"

"Yeah, but not nearly at the clip *I* was able to grow revenue here over the past five years."

"How are you paying these people?"

"Competitive base salaries plus commissions. Hey, they can make a lot of money if they score some touchdowns. They have everything to gain. I just can't understand why they are not hitting their targets."

"What targets? Whose targets?"

"My targets. I set them, and believe me, I wouldn't ask any of them to do anything I don't do every day of my life."

"Have you lost any sales people?"

"Yes, damn it. I train them, then they get nabbed by other companies. Really *!@!* me off! But, hey, I'm talking too much. What do you think?"

Mr. Shmooze shot a quick glance at me. He knew that Irving was just getting started. "Irv, I have some thoughts, but what do *you* think?" As Mr. Shmooze predicted, Irving was still rolling.

"I think I can't find anybody with the same passion, the same fire in their belly, as I have. No matter how hard I push these guys, they don't seem to get it. I want them to live and die with the business the way I do, every hour of every day. That's the way you sell this stuff!"

"Kid," Mr. Shmooze said, "How can anyone argue with that? I told you Irv was the most passionate businessman I had ever met." Irving sat up even straighter and basked in the compliment. "Irv, what is your profit margin?"

"8.765 percent!"

"Could you be a little more precise, please?" Irving laughed, we all laughed.

"Let's see—8.765 percent on sales of $50 million. So you're dropping—"

"$4,382,000!" interrupted Irving.

"—to the bottom line. That's phenomenal. Any partners?"

"Yeah—my wife and kids!"

"Wow, and I suppose you are taking a decent salary and some nice perks out of the deal before profits?"

"Not *that* much," Irving said. "I pay myself a salary of $500,000, a car and a couple of country clubs."

"A car...." Shmooze queried.

"Okay, a 450 SL."

"No plane?"

"I time share a King Air," smiled Irving, obviously glad he was asked.

"So, let's say you're pulling $5 million out of the operation. First of all, congratulations! See, kid," Mr. Shmooze said to me, "this is what can happen when someone has a good idea, works hard and believes in himself. And this is a real overnight success story, right Irv? What did it take you to build this up—two, three years?"

I thought Irving was going to come right over the conference table.

"Two or three years!?! I've been at this day and night for 14

*%@# years! You think this was *easy*? In the first two years I oper-
ated out of my garage at home. The same big question every two
weeks was if I could make payroll or not. You see these fingernails?
These are what I was hanging by for months on end!"

"I hear you, but you are the best salesman I know. It must not
have taken you long to start landing business!"

"Bull*%@#. I worked 18 hours a day, called on everyone,
worked all my relationships. I couldn't close a thing. Even my
friends didn't help. They were polite, but nobody was doing me any
big favors."

"How did you break through?"

"Persistence. I just kept hammering and, eventually, I got one
job, then two, then four. Once I got some momentum going, I had
some referrals, gained some confidence and all the hard work
began to pay off."

"So you began to do well, when?"

"About three years into the program."

"And you began to really succeed…"

"Okay, five or six years… hey! Wait a minute. I think I see where
you're going with this, Shmooze." Again, Mr. Shmooze glanced
quickly at me, then back to Irving.

"What do you mean?"

"Well, here I am, complaining that my salespeople are not hitting
their stride yet, even though it took me three years to make a profit and five years to kick some butt! Wait a second—I started from
scratch and these guys have a platform!"

"A platform, really? What kind of platform?"

"You know, a going business, a service, a brand name!"

"In Charlotte?"

"Well, not exactly. I mean, when they book some business, we
are ready to perform!"

"Just like when you started. You were ready to perform then, too,
right?"

"Well, yeah. But these guys have the benefit of my experience."

"Your experience? You mean your selling experience?"

"Absolutely. I am always open for training, communication. In fact, I will fly anywhere for a presentation if they need me."

"What do you tell them? That is, what has your experience taught you?"

"That this is a relationship business, damn it. I succeeded by building relationships, day and night, every day, day-in and day-out."

"So, the 'platform' is really a platform of relationships?"

"Absolutely!"

"And you or, say, you and your salesperson have not developed as many relationships in Charlotte over the past two years as you have in Atlanta over the past fourteen years. But that you expect him or her to match your success here in Atlanta at this point?"

For the first time, Irving didn't have a response. Mr. Shmooze seized the opportunity and waded in. "But if, by good fortune, your salesperson—by the way, what's his name?"

"Denise."

"Sorry! Denise. If Denise could build a book of business like you have in Atlanta, she can make—what did we say—$5 million a year?"

"Are you nuts? She can make $150,000, $200,000 tops. A great living!"

"Agreed! But didn't you say earlier you were frustrated that you could not find someone *just like yourself*? Fire in the belly, all that?"

"Exactly. These kids today don't get it."

"Don't get what?"

"They don't want to make the kind of commitment I do! Don't want to make a sacrifice."

"Irv, Irv, *Irv*! My friend. My good man. If we held a nationwide search, right now, for the next Irving, and she had exactly your intelligence, drive, ego, passion, talent and commitment, in other words, *you* fourteen years ago, do you think she would be satisfied with $150,000 per year? Do you think she would work *for* anybody? Irv, think about it! Put yourself in her shoes. What do you think she would do?"

Irving grumbled. "Start her own business. @*!*!!"

"Irv, don't feel bad. It is impossible to achieve the success you have realized without the kind of white-hot drive that men and women like you have. If you did not have such drive, we wouldn't be having this conversation! But when it becomes time to grow beyond that which you can see, feel and touch yourself, or even time to exit for that matter, you only have two options: One, share enough to attract true clones. Or two, lower your expectations and provide a reasonable environment in which less-driven people can succeed—for themselves first and for you second. Irv, I can sit here and pontificate forever on the classic mismatch between owners' expectations and employees' performance. But you're a numbers guy and you know your own world like nobody else. Do you want to build a quick case study to prove a point?"

"Let's do it."

"How many years did you say it took you to start really rocking in Atlanta?"

"Three."

"How many to—I'm talking about feeling good and having fun."

"I think he said five," I offered. Irving froze me with a glare, then lightened up and said, "He's right, about five." I felt my gut relax as I clumsily reached for a glass of water.

"And once you hit the five-year mark, how fast did you grow?" Irving brightened up like a man remembering hitting a game-winning home run.

"Oh, baby, we started doubling our business! We actually had to turn away some accounts. It was great."

"Any idea about, say, average growth over the years?"

"Oh, 25, 30 percent."

"Kid, pull out your calculator. Start with year five, at the five-year mark of…" Mr. Shmooze looked at Irving for the number.

"Five million," Irving said.

"…of $5 million. Calculate Irving's growth rate from year five, when he was doing $5 million in revenue, to year fourteen, when he was doing $50 million in revenue." I was already on it.

"That's an average of 38 percent per year," I offered gamely.

"So, Irving, you are hiring new entrepreneurs who, by definition, are nothing like you, paying them, what—three percent of what you make? Asking them to open a new city and begin matching your average growth rate of *38 percent* immediately—even though it took you, 'The King,' five years to do so in the first place. What's wrong with this picture?"

"Wrong salesperson?" said Irving.

"Maybe. What else?"

"Wrong compensation?"

"Probably."

"Wrong expectations?"

"Absolutely."

"So, I'm cooked and should close my satellite offices?"

"Of course not. What we need to do is *calibrate* the salesperson, the compensation and the expectations, with something fair, reasonable and, ultimately, productive to everyone concerned. Each element plays off the other. But it all starts with your expectations."

"What do you mean?"

"Well, is your goal for this business to be a cash cow, or do you want to build equity?"

"The answer is yes!"

Mr. Shmooze turned to me and grinned. "Why does that not surprise me? But, Irv, you know what I mean."

"Well, cash has always been king. Now I am trying to expand, create critical mass and get some leverage under the business."

"IPO?"

"Maybe. But, in any case, I will be more attractive to investors if I am geographically diverse and larger in general."

"Irv, you run a service business, a great service business. In manufacturing, how do you think a company grows?"

"They invest in plant, equipment and increase capacity and output."

"How do they measure the success of such a plan?" Irving thought for a moment.

"I would assume they measure a return on their investment."

"In your service business, in Charlotte, what is the nature of your investment?"

"Denise."

"Forgetting your own, super-human sales achievements as the one-off superstar owner/entrepreneur, what would you deem to be a reasonable annual return on your investment in Denise, versus the opportunity to invest your profits in, say, stocks and bonds?" Irving stopped, thinking hard. His eyes narrowed.

Finally, he offered, "20 percent or so."

"Okay, so if you are paying Denise $150,000 per year to receive a 20 percent return on your investment, she would need to cover her compensation and a profit of $30,000 to hit the 20 percent mark. Kid, at a margin of 8.75 percent, what kind of gross revenue does Denise have to hit to drop $30,000 into Irving's pocket?" My fingers were flying as Mr. Shmooze was talking. I had the answer by the end of his sentence.

"$342,857."

"So, Denise needs to sell $150,000 to cover her costs and another $192,857 to yield a 20 percent overall return, that is she needs to total $342,857 in gross revenue to hit her mark. Irv, how did she do last year?"

"She sold around $400,000."

"So you have a huge winner on your hands!! Congratulations!"

"But *I* could sell—"

"It does not matter what you could sell! *She is not you!* She is a $150,000-caliber salesperson. She returns over 20 percent on your investment, cash on cash. And we are not even considering the value she is building under your business. If the multiple is four or five times, then she is a *great* investment."

"Well, if you put it that way…"

"Irv, that is the only way. Read my lips, old buddy: *You get what you pay for.* Work the math. You want to make 25 percent on your investment? Take a bigger risk. Hire a $200,000-caliber salesperson. You want to match your success in Atlanta? Franchise your business and find clones to run the franchises. But stop beating the crap out of $150,000 salespeople for not producing triple-digit returns in this context. If you do, as you said yourself, you might as well be in the sales-training business for your competitors."

Irving rose to his feet. "Kid," he said, "I love this guy! Now, what did we decide again?"

"We didn't decide anything, but I think we have shown that it is reasonable and fair to recruit and incentivize salespeople through a return on investment formula. The trick will be for you to dig deep and decide what your real goals are, then match the caliber of your salespeople with those goals. Twenty percent seems to be reasonable for a $150,000 salesperson in this context. Matching your own skill level is *not*, and you will break your own heart—not to mention hers—trying to do so."

Mr. Shmooze stood up. "Tell you what. Send me your numbers for the two new offices, along with your sales reps' compensation since being hired. I'll go over them with my friend, Stan Lanier, over at Compensation Specialists. Let's meet again next week."

As we were leaving, Mr. Shmooze turned to Colleen and handed her a book on dealing with aging parents. They shared a knowing look and she got up, came around her desk and gave him a hug.

Chapter Six
"THE LEGEND"

One evening, when I happened to drop by the Clubhouse, a new watering hole in the Buckhead area, I bumped into Ed Morris and a group of heavyweight real estate types who invited me over for a drink. Ed introduced me to the gang.

"Hey, guys, this is Shmooze's intern for the summer." I shook some hands, high-fived a few others. But I had a funny feeling I was being drawn into the proverbial barrel.

"Where is the Shmooze man tonight?" one of them asked.

"He's on a plane to New York," I said, "so I actually have a few hours to myself." Naturally, at that precise moment, the phone rang and it was Mr. Shmooze calling from the plane.

"Kid, I just talked to Jerry Warner. Meet him at the Ritz tomorrow morning at 7:30 and drop off those reports we talked about this morning."

"No problem," I said.

The crowd chimed in, "Is that Shmooze? Ask him if he is going out with Trump tonight in Manhattan!"

"Yeah, and tell him to say 'hello' to Hillary for us!"

I switched on my cell phone's speaker function, just as Shmooze countered, "Ask those guys what the difference is between a real estate broker and a hooker. Answer? Real estate brokers have a license!"

Immediately, I was pelted with ice and profanities as both sides laughed at my having been shot as the messenger. Moments later, Shmooze was gone and I was left on my own with the riled up brokers. Rich Hammond, an ultra-successful Atlanta developer, then began what turned out to be a solid hour of Mr. Shmooze stories.

"Shmooze and I had done some business and broken bread together," Rich said, "but he was not one of my closest friends at the time. It was my wedding day, and believe it or not, I get a call *in the church*, while I am waiting with my best man in the guests' changing room! There were no cell phones back then, so Shmooze had gone to the trouble of figuring out the church's name and phone number, not to mention the date and time of my wedding.

"So the Pastor's secretary tells me I have a call. When I answer, there's Mr. Shmooze wishing me a great day and a happy and healthy life and marriage! It was terrific. I'll never forget it."

"I know what you mean," said David, a big-time tenant representative sporting a $10,000 Rolex. "One night, I bumped into Mr. Shmooze at a huge awards banquet. You know, one of those things where you can barely hear and you have about ten seconds to talk to everyone. I was all excited because my daughter's soccer team had advanced to the state quarterfinals and I mentioned to a group that included Shmooze that I was going to take the next day off to go to the game. I didn't have a chance to elaborate the where and when, but sure enough, right before the opening kick, I feel two hands on my shoulders, and who do you think is sitting right behind me? Mr. Shmooze! We lived and died together through that whole game. And when Katherine's team won in overtime on a penalty kick, we went crazy! Screaming and jumping up and down. It was one of the happiest days of my life, and Shmooze was right in the middle of it!"

"Well how about this," said Don Jackson. "I'm in Las Vegas at a seminar and Shmooze is the host. It's early and everybody's pretty sleepy, not to mention hung over. There are meetings happening on either side of us and the walls are thin enough so you can occasionally hear applause in nearby rooms. Mr. Shmooze takes command and says, 'Come on, let's shake things up! On the count of three, everybody burst into applause and laugh like crazy for ten seconds. Watch what happens.' So, at the count of three, we all whooped it up and laughed for five seconds, then ten seconds. Now we're all laughing for real and the adrenaline begins to flow and the situation becomes genuinely funny.

"Sure enough, heads started popping in the door. 'What's going on here?' 'What's so funny?' 'Hell, your guys are having fun! I'm staying!' Needless to say, our session was the talk of the day. We shook out the cobwebs and it was easy to buy into Mr. Shmooze's first topic—'Positive Vibes Are Contagious.'"

"Oh, man, I have seen Shmooze do that a thousand times at games, golf outings, bars," added Ed. "He will walk into a place like this when it's quiet and within an hour he's got two bartenders, three waitresses, five friends and ten strangers hanging around, laughing. I asked him about it once and he said, 'You see all the people sitting around here doing nothing? I'm drawing all the energy they're too afraid to use and channeling it into our group.' He called it the Vortex Effect."

"Another time," said Rich Hammond, "We were planning an awards dinner and we wanted to figure out how to give away a car for impact. Someone said, 'Too bad it's winter, or we could have a hole-in-one contest.' Shmooze jumps in and says, 'Great idea! Let's make it a putting contest! We can get an insurance company to underwrite the whole thing.' Sure enough, we ended up with a 55-foot putting contest plus a $60,000 Lexus for a prize, and an insurance company underwrote the whole thing. It was the talk of the town all winter."

"Listen to this. I'm in a presentation with Shmooze," said Jim. "We are pitching the management and leasing for a sixty-story building in Chicago. We are up against all the top firms and the audience is a group of tough, New York investment banking types. We are last to go and it's about 5 p.m. Chicago time, 6 p.m. New York time. We walk in, exchange pleasantries, then Shmooze reaches down and brings up two six-packs of Heineken, which he slams down on the table! 'Folks,' he says, 'I know you're tired and all of these presentations are running together. It's cocktail hour in Manhattan. Why don't we kick back, have a beer and, instead of having you listen to another boring pitch, let's just shoot the bull about how we are going to lease your building together.' From then on, through further presentations and well after we had won the assignment, they always called us The Heineken Guys!"

"Speaking of Heineken, do any of you guys know why bartenders and waitresses like Mr. Shmooze so much?" asked David.

"Because he's a big tipper!" yelled our bartender, who was hovering nearby.

"Very subtle, George," said Jim. "I'm sure that's true, but the real secret is that he actually engages them and even helps them out at some point. You know, many people in those positions are going to school to land a completely different kind of job."

"That's right," Ed added. "Shmooze always listens and often follows up with contacts or advice that help these folks elevate their game!"

"I can testify to that," said the bartender. "We had a lady here who was trying to break into public relations. Before you knew it, Shmooze had arranged a couple of interviews for her. Now she's an intern at Hill and Knowlton, and one of Mr. Shmooze's key contacts in the public relations world."

While the stories went on and on, Ed quietly took me aside and said, "This guy has reached out and touched a lot of people. But he does more than just touch them; he adds *value* to their day-to-day lives. He always gives more than he gets. Don't ever forget that."

Chapter Seven
SIMPLY NETWORKING MEANS NOTHING

"It must be tough to wade through such a large database. I guess that's the price you pay for being the world's greatest networker." Mr. Shmooze and I had stopped for a rare visit to his office. He was scanning his database on a laptop when I decided to make what I thought would be a complimentary observation. Shmooze looked up.

"What did you say?"

"I said, you are the world's greatest networker. You know, 500,000 contacts, all that stuff."

Mr. Shmooze was now fully focused on me. He got up. "Follow me," he said. We went into a conference room together. Mr. Shmooze closed the door, then, turning to me, he continued. "Kid, I can see that I have failed to emphasize one of the most important points during our talks about marketing and selling. *Simply networking means nothing.*"

"But—" I began. Mr. Shmooze put his hand up to silence me. He spoke slowly and deliberately.

"Simply networking means nothing. Think about it for a second before responding."

I was a little exasperated at that moment. "I'm confused," I said. "For the past three weeks I have watched you interact with an endless stream of people in a variety of venues. Everyone from carhops to CEOs. You reach out and touch them, cultivate them, make them feel great. With all due respect—I thought networking was your life—or, at least, a big part of it."

"Kid, I understand why you might reach that conclusion. And it is true that, in order to do what I do, you need to establish a network of people. But here's my point: It's not about the quantity of your relationships, it's about the quality of your relationships. It's about *adding value through your relationships!* Believe it or not, I know account representatives at ad agencies who make over a million dollars a year attending to—get this—*one client.* That's right! Their whole business life revolves around servicing one customer very, very well. The key is to figure out how many really deep relationships you need to have in order to succeed and to put 90 percent of your energy into developing the quality of those specific relationships."

"Then why do you expend so much time and energy on everyone else?"

"Because everyone else helps me service my top relationships," Mr. Shmooze answered, "and vice-versa. And because it's fun! But let's stick with quality over quantity. Here is how I do it." Mr. Shmooze walked to a mahogany panel and slid it back to reveal a blackboard. "I start out with a scale of one to five. A 'one' is someone I barely know. A 'five' would take a bullet for me and vice-versa. Literally.

"Now I create a simple graph. This represents my business relationships. My livelihood. On the left side, I again rate the personal relationship from one to five. On the right side, I rate the person's ability to impact my business. Obviously, I have some dear friends who rate a high five personally, but who have no impact on my business. I also know some CEOs who rank five in business, but with whom I have little contact. In the business context, the best scenario is—"

"Tens! That is, people you know intimately with whom you also do business!"

"Right on! Actually, to be realistic, my goal is to maintain eights, nines and tens with as many people as I can at any given time."

"What happens if someone retires, or whatever?"

"Then I move someone else up. Every week I rate as many relationships as I can. The name of the game is upward progress for everyone, but intense focus on my top tier."

"But don't you need to establish a network to address in the first place?"

"Of course. In my classes I say, 'Simply networking is nothing,' just to make a dramatic point. But remember this: The landscape is littered with the bones of bright young salespeople who spent countless hours building a huge database of low-rated relationships on their fancy laptops.

"Let's look at it another way. A lot of sales trainers will teach that it takes 100 calls to get 10 meetings to make one sale. If that's true, then one good relationship is 100 times more important than 99 casual encounters. Yet many people will treat that precious resource with neglect, spending endless time making still another 100 calls, searching for the next contact, even as hungry thieves are picking their pockets. Kid, good relationships are very rare, very precious. Once you have one, your top priority must be to nurture, grow and protect it…with your life."

Chapter Eight
WAR WHOOPS FROM THE MANAGERS

The next day, Mr. Shmooze and I found ourselves on the highway heading to the world headquarter of a major soft drink company. It was a gathering of its sales managers from around the country and Mr. Shmooze was the featured speaker the first morning of the meeting.

"These folks are really smart," said Shmooze, sipping coffee as he maneuvered into the shared ride lane. "Most companies concentrate their training on their sales people. Very few of them understand how important it is to also support the sales managers. Coaches need training, too! Hell, we all need help from time to time."

Before I knew it, we were on a stage facing about a hundred predominantly type-A sales managers. Needless to say, their tables were filled with various soft drink products. One thing stood out, however. At each chair a book by Daniel Goleman had been placed, called Emotional Intelligence. A ribbon was placed around it, that read, "Please do not open."

"Ladies and Gentlemen, welcome to our annual meeting of sales managers. Thank you so much for making the commitment to come and share ideas with us and with each other." The emcee went on for several more minutes before introducing Mr. Shmooze with the words, "We would like to open the meeting by spending some time with a man many of you already know. He has told me that he will help each of us make more money and have more fun doing it, guaranteed! Here is…Mr. Shmooze!" Mr. Shmooze strode confidently to the center of the stage, surrounded by warm applause. As always, he smiled broadly and made eye contact with as many individuals as he could.

"What a pleasure it is to be standing before the people who have created one of the most recognized brands in the world!" He was nearly shouting. "In fact—stand up and give yourselves a hand for this absolutely unique accomplishment." People around the room began to stand up. "C'mon—this is an amazing feat, and *you* did it! Be excited! Be proud!" I watched as one by one every person in the room stood up and began clapping, high-fiving, and shouting together enthusiastically. It was amazing! "Yeah!" said Mr. Shmooze.

"I love talking to sales managers!" he continued. "You know why? Because they are combat veterans. They earned their stripes on the street. They are the best of the best. And because they always keep their massive egos in check and are open to new ideas!" Suddenly, a huge message came up on two large screens positioned on each end of the stage: "LAUGHTER OPENS MINDS."

Shmooze paused for a moment and let everyone stop laughing to absorb the message. Then he said, "Folks, today we are going to talk about building and supporting a *great* sales team. And we are going to do it by covering *five* key points. Every time we hit a key point, we are going to demonstrate it, talk about it and review it. Bang, bang, bang. This is the way the best teachers teach and the best students learn. And this is how you should approach the coaching of your sales force.

"Point number one. Make them laugh! Sound trite? Think about this. I put a book on your table called Emotional Intelligence, by Daniel Goleman. It talks about the huge part emotions play in life and I will refer to it often today. Here is what Goleman says about laughter:

> Good moods... enhance the ability to think flexibly and with more complexity, thus making it easier to find solutions to problems.... This suggests that one way to help someone think through a problem is to tell him a joke. Laughing, like elation, seems to help people think more broadly and associate more freely, noticing relationships that might have eluded otherwise.... One study found that people who had just watched a video of TV bloopers were better at solving a puzzle long used by psychologists to test creative thinking.

At that moment the screens switched to an obvious TV blooper. Again, everybody laughed, long and hard.

"You see, Goleman explains that memory is 'state-specific.' Your people will remember better if they associate the memory with a good mood. I will emphasize this point more in a few minutes." The screen was doused to black. "MAKE THEM LAUGH" came up.

"Folks, Ronald Reagan was famous for great storytelling. He started nearly every important meeting with his staff, with new acquaintances, even with Gorbachev, with a story to loosen everyone up. Start your sales meetings the same way. Teach your people to do it with their customers. Need stories?" The screen changed and "www.joke.com" appeared. "There are dozens of Web sites. Use this tool. It works. Guaranteed!

"Now, I went a little bit out of order to get the meeting rolling. Let's back up a second. In fact, let's go back to the first thing we need to build a great team." Mr. Shmooze clicked to a picture of the Atlanta Braves. "Help me out. Anyone, what is the first thing we need to build a championship team like the Atlanta Braves?"

"Greg Maddux!" shouted one manager, getting into the spirit of laughter.

"You're on the right track," Shmooze replied. "Broaden it."

"Superstars!" yelled another.

"That's right! But, before they were superstars, they were..."

"Good draft choices!"

"Bingo! The man in blue is right on. The first thing the Braves need to build a great baseball team is people who can pitch and hit a baseball. The first thing your company needs to build a great sales team is people who can *sell*. Or, more especially for new recruits, people who have the *potential* to be great salespeople!

"And what do you think is the number-one indicator that a person will succeed as a salesperson?" Answers flew around the room from all directions: "Grit!" "Intelligence!" "Determination!" "Persistence!" "Guts!" "Happy disposition!" Shmooze wheeled around and walked toward the woman who yelled the last answer.

"Did you say happy?" he asked.

"Yes! A happy disposition."

"You are all over it! Let me refine your point a little. If someone is not a pessimist, she is an—"

"Optimist!" shouted the crowd.

"Right on. Why do you think that is the number-one indicator of a person's potential to succeed as a salesperson?

"Because salespeople face rejection every day," came a woman's voice from the center of the room. "If you are not an optimist, the profession can grind you down."

"Ladies and Gentlemen, did you know you had a genius among you?" said Mr. Shmooze. "Stand up and take a bow." The woman stood up, to healthy applause. Meanwhile, the screen split, displaying a happy face next to a sad one. "Sound basic? Goleman tells us something that absolutely blows my mind. Listen, and listen very carefully.

"A psychologist by the name of Martin Seligman has tested both Olympic athletes and salespeople to correlate the impact of optimism on performance. He tested insurance salespeople at MetLife. Here is what Goleman says: 'Being able to take a rejection with grace is essential in sales of all kinds, especially with a product like life insurance, where the ratios of 'nos' to 'yeses' can be so discouragingly high. For this reason, about 75 percent of insurance sales-men quit in the first three years.'

"However, Goleman says that Seligman found that new sales-men—who were, by nature, *optimists*—sold 37 percent more insur-ance in their first two years on the job than did pessimists. And, during the first year, the pessimists quit at twice the rate of the opti-mists. Now here's the real payoff!

"Goleman writes that Seligman persuaded MetLife to hire a spe-cial group of applicants who scored high on a test for optimism—but get this!—*failed* the normal screening tests. This special group of optimists outsold the others by 21 percent in their first year, 57 percent in the second." The statistics appeared on the screen, superimposed over a happy or sad face, respectively. Shmooze looked at the group and held his arms wide, hands palms up.

"Would the Braves or Yankees ever hire someone who couldn't hit? Of course not. Yet companies hire hundreds of thousands of pessimists every year, people who may have many other fine skills, but who do not have a *prayer* competing against optimists in the rough and tumble world of selling." The screen went black, and the title "RECRUIT OPTIMISTS" appeared. "Ladies and Gentlemen, recruit optimists. And not by intuition, not by chance. Test for it. And send the pessimists over to your competitors!" War whoops and a huge applause echoed through the crowd. The room was qui-eted by old newsreel footage on the screens.

"You know, many people rate Franklin Delano Roosevelt as one of our greatest presidents," Mr. Shmooze said. "He was paraplegic, yet served four terms, first through the Great Depression then through WWII, arguably the most stressful periods of the twentieth century. You know what Oliver Wendell Holmes said about FDR? That he was a giant, but not because he was especially smart. Holmes said FDR had a second-class intellect but a first-class dis-position. FDR was the grandfather of all optimists at precisely the time our country most needed one.

"This brings me to our next, related topic. Did you know that people can be *trained* to be optimistic? No, I'm not contradicting myself—you are still better off as sales managers recruiting natural optimists. But there are obviously degrees involved. And people can actually *improve* this key component of their personality. Watch this!" Mr. Shmooze turned toward the screens. A video flashed to life. It was of the Chicago Bulls, led by six-time world champion, Michael Jordan.

In the video, Jordan talked about his tough early years in the league, how, through persistence, steady improvement and skill, he and his teammates developed the 'habit of winning.' Jordan said that once they started winning, they expected to win, and the confidence fed off itself, lifting each player higher and higher to his best level as an individual and, ultimately, to six world championships as a team. The image faded and up came the words: "THE HABIT OF WINNING."

"Folks, one of the single biggest mistakes I see sales managers make, with both new recruits and seasoned veterans, is signing them up, turning them loose and saying, 'Go out there and make money!' The salespeople put on their helmets, run out the door and proceed to get the 'you-know-what' kicked out of them. They begin to develop fear and a habit of losing. One of the most valuable things you can do for a salesperson is to occasionally provide a friendly contact, a warm lead, and in the case of a younger salesperson, call on the prospects with him or her. Let them get the taste of winning in their mouths. And reinforce that taste.

"In fact, try this one and have some fun with it. Occasionally, I will call one of my regular customers and set up an opportunity for a salesperson to close him. We'll both go, but I will sit back and let my protégé do the work. My customer will put him through the paces, all right, but it's basically a *fait accompli*.

"A bit contrived? Of course. But my protégé gets the win on *his* sales report. He has something to brag about at the tavern after work and to his fiancée at dinner on Saturday night. He wakes up the next morning a little earlier, walks a little taller and works a little harder. Ladies and Gentlemen—don't just cut them loose and tell them to go out and sell. That's not what the Braves do. Work with your people. Build up their confidence. Optimism is contagious! Hey, speaking of contagious, watch this!"

The video screens again came alive and the room was filled with thumping rock music. It was the Beatles playing before 50,000 wildly screaming fans at Shea Stadium. The band was laughing and really rocking. The camera pans the crowd for close-ups of kids laughing, crying, having a great time. It was impossible not to get into a good mood as the video played on. One screen continued to show the concert, the other flashed the next point in huge letters: "FEELINGS ARE CONTAGIOUS."

"Ladies and Gentlemen, why do you think people gravitate toward rock concerts, ball games, the theater? Just shout out some answers."

"To see and hear a great performance," someone said.

"True enough, although he could probably see and hear a great performance on TV or a CD. Can you refine your point a little?"

"To *experience* a great performance," said a voice next to the first one.

"Man, you people are smart! 'Experience a great performance.' Absolutely, positively the right answer. And why do you suppose experiencing a great performance with other people is even better than experiencing it by yourself?"

From the corner someone shouted, "Because you can *share* the experience."

"That's right. And the reason human beings can share experiences is because *feelings are contagious.* And when feelings are shared, people's feelings can get stronger and stronger, even to a point of frenzy. Psychologists call this phenomenon 'effervescence.' Think about your own home towns. What happened in Chicago when the Bears won the Super Bowl? Or in LA when the Lakers won the NBA championship? Man, you all talked about it for days, weeks, months!

"There is enormous power in this phenomenon. Enormous potential. But there is also a dark side, a mirror image we have to think about. Some of us are old enough to remember how we felt when JFK died. We all remember how devastated we were when Challenger went down. We showed those feelings, too. You folks are managers and by definition, that means you are leaders. As leaders, you hold enormous power. *You* set the tone for your people. *You* develop the emotional climate. Your feelings are contagious.

"I can't tell you how many sales managers say to me, 'It's a war out there. My job is to beat the hell out of my people. If they can't face me, how can they face the customer?' Ladies and Gentlemen, I once monitored all e-mail for one of my consulting clients for three months, and the negative vibes coming from the 'command and control' manager were devastating!" Phrases flashed on one screen or the other, as Mr. Shmooze spoke them aloud: "You're way behind." "You're not hitting your numbers." "You're way off budget." "Your expense report is fishy."

"Folks, there is a time and a place for using both a stick and a carrot. There is certainly room for financial discipline and for facing production facts. But too many sales managers use bad vibes to hide their own insecurity, to make sure everyone knows who's in charge. The costs to teamwork, morale and production are incredible. Your basic job as a leader in the sales context is to *invigorate* and *lift* the spirits of your team. Remember, salespeople can work anywhere. They want to be with you because, while things may be tough on the street or things may be tough at home, at work there is hope, pride, dignity and optimism." These words flashed on the screen, with 'optimism' lingering in big, bold letters. "Work provides good friends, good vibes and supportive leadership. It may not be a Beatles concert. However, for the most part, the shared feelings at the office should be upbeat and optimistic.

"All right folks. Today we have talked about the power of emotion in the context of your world as sales managers. Let's review for a minute." The screen cut to black and up came four boxes, numbered one through four. The first box filled in right away, and Mr. Shmooze reiterated the words, LAUGHTER OPENS MINDS. "This is not touchy-feely stuff," he said. "It is a physiological fact. A little laughter goes a long way in relaxing people, releasing favorable chemicals in their brains and opening up the creative pathways in people's minds."

The second box was filled and Mr. Shmooze said, "RECRUIT OPTIMISTS. And I mean *real* optimists. People can fake optimism and undermine the team behind the scenes. And real optimists can have bad interviews. The only way to know for sure is to test them, in advance. Optimists will sell better and make more money for everyone!"

The third box was filled. "DEVELOP THE HABIT OF WINNING," Mr. Shmooze said. "Your job is to develop winners. That means coaching, mentoring and supporting. And get out there with them. Phil Jackson does not ride a desk. He is on the court teaching, in the locker room supporting!"

Then the last box was filled. "EMOTIONS ARE CONTAGIOUS," said Mr. Shmooze. "You are a leader. Your emotions are most important to your team. If you are upbeat, your people will follow. If you are sour, your team won't stand a chance.

"If you enjoy acting like George Patton, beating up and scaring the devil out of your troops—showing everyone who is in charge— here is my advice: Join the Army. Despite what others may have told you, selling is *not* warfare. It is not life or death! You know the trouble with that philosophy? It causes you to pick fights with everyone, including your customers. And you may not even know you're doing it! Don't get me wrong. It's okay to declare war on your competition. But the way to win that war is to develop positive mentoring and, yes, a nurturing *esprit de corps*, which washes over into your sales meetings, your sales calls and your customer relationships.

"Let's close today with one final lesson. When your salespeople charge out of their next sales meetings and call in on their next customers, what should be their top objective? Anyone?"

"Close!"

"Produce!"

"Build the relationship!"

"All well and good," Mr. Shmooze agreed. "All in good time. Remember, the accent today is on emotions. So what can a salesperson accomplish *every time* with every person?"

"They can make the prospect feel good!"

"You folks don't need me! He's right! Dale Carnegie 101. Advertisers call it a 'love bite.' It is the absolute key to selling. Think about it. Your buyer gets up in the morning and, from dawn until dusk, will experience literally thousands of stimuli at home, on the road, from the paper, the TV, the radio, meetings, spouse, kids, whatever. The buyer's mood will have to sift through thousands of bits of information to find that which he deems to be meaningful. Time works ferociously against him.

"Here you come, Mr. or Ms. Super Salesperson, briefcase in hand, smile on your face. When you walk in his door, one of two things is *guaranteed* to happen: Either you will interrupt him, causing a negative response before immediately fading into the deep, blurred oblivion of 100,000 other colorless stimuli he is processing that day, or you will elicit a special, positive emotion, a good feeling, the type of feeling that his brain will gently extract from the general information flow and, with tender care, move it over to the special, warm place in his mind where time slows down, where smiles are created, where trust is born. The good memory place. And, people, there is one and only one way to take your message to this sacred hunting ground. Remember, it cannot get in on its own. It must ride in on a good emotion. A pleasing experience. A good vibration.

"Ladies and Gentlemen, when you call on a new prospect or a precious, existing customer, no matter what else happens, whether she is ready to buy, is distracted, is stonewalling, whatever—just make sure one thing happens: When she thinks of you, she thinks of something good. Something warm. Add, somehow, to her day. How? By giving her something. Information. A small gift. A compliment from a peer. A thousand ways. I have left some ideas for you to read later.

"If you like mission statements, here is your mission. When you walk out that prospect's door, his or her conscious and unconscious mind must say, 'Good guy. Glad he stopped by. Added to my day. Got me thinking. I feel a little better now than before he showed up.' Follow that up with a little card, an appropriate follow-up. Again. Again. Gently at first. Keep knocking at the good vibe door. Soon enough, the guard dog inside will step aside and, once you're in, you and your newfound friend can take the relationship wherever you mutually want it to go. And, by the way, you might just be able to sell something while you're at it!

"Bye folks!! Thank you for your time!"

Chapter Nine
THE THEATRE OF LIFE

It was nearing the end of my last day and I could not believe my luck. The busiest man I had ever met, Mr. Shmooze, had invited me to dinner, alone, and I was on the way to meet him where it all started—the Ritz Carlton Hotel.

By now I knew everyone at the hotel and was a member of the family: Rudy, the car attendant; Joe, the doorman; and Susan, the hostess. Tonight, however, was the first time I was going to eat upstairs at the famous Ritz Restaurant. I was really pumped up. At the entranceway, I was welcomed by a very dignified-looking maître d'.

"Ah, you must be Robert, the young man Mr. Shmooze is waiting for. Follow me." As we wound our way through the beautiful restaurant, serene music played in the background and people talked quietly. I scanned the best tables looking for Mr. Shmooze. My eyes had not yet adjusted to the lowered lighting, and, I could not make him out at any of the likely locations. Finally, we reached the back of the majestic room and the maître d' opened a swinging door.

"After you, sir," he said.

As the door swung closed behind us, I was suddenly bombarded by the most raucous combination of light, noise, energy and activity I had ever seen. What a scene! We were in the kitchen! And in the middle of the mêlée, apron and all, stood Mr. Shmooze, busily chopping onions.

"Hey, kid, over here! We're cooking tonight!" With that, I felt an arm around me, walking me toward the chopping block and taking off my coat. It was Joseph, the head chef.

"Correction. *I'm* cooking, he's 'helping,' you're learning. Then we will eat."

"Tony," said Mr. Shmooze, addressing the wine steward, "Pour Robert some wine. Robert, listen and learn!"

"Young man, this is a 1995 Chardonnay from the Russian River Valley in Northern California. It is a great wine to order before a gourmet dinner. It is light and will not destroy your taste buds. But remember: 1995 or 1996. Anything later is not ready to drink. Oh—and women love this wine."

"Now *that's* benefit-selling!" Mr. Shmooze chimed in. I sipped the wine as I stepped beside Mr. Shmooze at the worktable. Chef Joseph was hollering at one of his assistants for putting too much garlic in a salad.

"Too much! Too much! Why are you so ham-handed? This isn't Bennigan's, you know. Balance! Balance!" I couldn't quite tell how mad he really was, but his staff seemed to know. A few of them were hiding sly grins. This was obviously 'showtime', and they were all happy to be part of one of the most exciting restaurant experiences in the country. Joseph was the director and the star of the show. But everybody from busboy to waiter to assistant chef had key roles, and they were proud of it. Joseph, however, was just getting started.

"Gentlemen, welcome to my world. My home. My castle. Only one rule here: I am king, emperor, dictator. Listen to me and succeed. Contradict me and you are history! Tonight we will create great art, me by cooking, you by helping and sharing this most unique of experiences!"

Mr. Shmooze leaned over to me and whispered quietly, "He's quite full of himself."

"I heard that!" yelled Joseph, as he pointed toward the door.

"Sorry! Sorry!" stammered Mr. Shmooze, hiding his smile.

"Now let's get to work!" said Joseph. Over the next hour or so, between running what I came to understand to be the most complicated of operations, Joseph showed Mr. Shmooze and me how to prepare sautéed fois gras over baby greens, peppered lamb loin and truffled polenta. He was fantastic. His eyes and hands moved quickly and efficiently as he literally danced around the room, barking orders, gathering ingredients and preparing the food. Eventually Mr. Shmooze and I were led to a table in a corner of the kitchen that was just quiet enough to hold a solid conversation. The food and wine that came to us were, naturally, absolutely incredible.

"Robert, I have really enjoyed working with you this summer," said Mr. Shmooze as we finished our baked Alaskas. "Now, if you remember our sales calls, our meetings and our seminars, what always happens at the end?"

"You end on a high note! You leave a positive impression and elicit a positive emotion!"

"Beautiful! Just beautiful! And this is the last, most important lesson you are going to learn this summer. What do you think it is?"

"Well, come to think of it, I think Chef Joseph and his team embody lots of your lessons. He is passionate, proud. He seems very happy, even when he's ordering people around. His team follows his lead. Everyone is highly energized and focused."

Mr. Shmooze grinned widely and sipped some more wine. "Great, keep going."

"Come to think of it, I guess this is a microcosm of life in general: passion, commitment, leadership, optimism, energy." All of a sudden, Mr. Shmooze stood up and walked around the table to me. He pulled me to my feet and gave me an enormous hug, nearly lifting me out of my shoes.

"Kid," he said, like a proud father, "you have got it! You are going to be very, very special in life! You know," he said, sitting back down, "Henry David Thoreau once said that most people 'lead lives of quiet desperation.' Sounds depressing to me, but who knows, maybe that was the case years ago when it was all about simply surviving day-to-day. You know what I see as our modern-day dilemma? People *have* so much and the media exposes them *to* so much that they get caught up in a different trap. They want to do *everything*, be everywhere, lead scores of lives at the same time. They see Madonna and they want to be a rock star—Tom Cruise, and they want to be a movie star. But here is the simple little secret to a happy life: There is as much passion, pathos, energy and drama going on in this kitchen right now as in any movie Tom Cruise could ever make. Cruise knows it, too, that's why he is constantly on the lookout for a great, real story that he can 'act-out' through a film.

"Just look at Joseph." I looked over at Chef Joseph, wildly waving his arms around a flambé dish. "Late one night, years ago, he and I got pretty drunk together in the kitchen of a restaurant not too far from here—a different universe in terms of ambiance and quality. 'You know, Shmooze,' he told me, 'I hate being a chef. Don't get me wrong, I love cooking, but handling all of these people, running a kitchen, it is so boring. To me, it just distracts me from my art, my craft.'

"'Well,' I asked him, 'what would you be doing if you were not a chef?'

"'You know,' he said, 'I went to the symphony the other night, and the orchestra was playing beautifully. It was a complicated piece, with many highs and lows as well as a wide variety of transitions. I soon realized that the man holding it all together was the conductor. The artists' eyes were glued to him. In fact, many actually mirrored his facial expressions. When he grimaced, they grimaced. When he asked for volume or quiet, they delivered. He seemed so passionate, in command, energized—and happy!'

"'But Joseph,' I asked him, 'does a symphony have to involve musicians? Does a play have to involve an actual stage? Does a movie need a screen? He hadn't thought about it that way.'

"'You can literally have *every* experience and create *any* emotion in life right here in this kitchen,' I told him. 'Happiness, sadness, victory, defeat, passion—it's all here. This is your symphony.' Joseph was already a fine chef, a strong leader. What he needed to understand was that we can create passion anywhere and that it is *emotion*, not the setting, that is the key.

"Life is art and art is life. I'm a pretty good singer, but I sure can't draw a crowd like Frank Sinatra could. I like telling jokes, but nobody will ever mistake me for Bill Cosby. Yet, guess what? I can get every bit as high on life as they can and, when I'm riding that high, people come to me, just like they go to those people, to be part of the *glow*.

"Joseph is the Pavarotti of chefs. I am the Michael Jordan of marketing and sales consultants. There is a man outside who is the Fred Astaire of parking attendants, a woman in the spa who is the Oprah Winfrey of manicurists. We are all soul mates because we know the secret! And I will tell you something. Michael Jordan knows a soul mate when he sees one, whether it's an athlete, a chef or a carhop. And they absolutely love and respect each other for their common passion, no matter what their specialty or their position.

"Kid, my specialty is selling. Why am I fascinated with selling? Because selling is really the art and science of a much higher subject. The subject of life. *Everyone* communicates, listens, attempts to persuade, all day, every day of their lives. Yes, there are bad salespeople out there, just like there are bad politicians, journalists or lawyers. I am talking about decent people who are willing to work hard, learn their craft and sell for their living. There is no other profession that marries disposition and emotion with craft so closely.

There is no other career that allows one the opportunity to spread goodwill and get paid so handsomely for it. My God, think about it. Every morning, when I wake up, my mission is so clear! *The happier I can make myself, the happier I can make other people. The happier I can make other people, the more I get paid.* Talk about positive reinforcement! End of lesson! Any questions?"

"Only one, sir. Not all of us can be Mr. Shmooze. We cannot all be larger than life. Are you telling the rest of us to fake it?"

"No, no, no, no! Be honest! Be yourself! But push a little, stretch a little! Develop your own style."

Suddenly, the doors were thrust open and all of the folks I had met at the Ritz over the summer rushed in behind Joseph, who was carrying a large cake. They burst into an off-key, boisterous rendition of 'For He's A Jolly Good Fellow.' Mr. Shmooze and I rose to our feet, and there were lots of hugs and kisses all around. Naturally, Mr. Shmooze took the floor.

"Good friends, I propose a toast to young Robert Richards here, a.k.a. 'The Kid.' May he spread the word far and wide. Health, happiness and much love in his life."

"Hear, hear!"

Mr. Shmooze pulled out a Dunhill cigar and put his arm around me. "Now, unless Joseph has changed his kitchen rules..." said Mr. Shmooze, glancing sideways at his old friend. In response, Joseph picked up a large meat cleaver and headed right for Mr. Shmooze. "I didn't think so. Then I will meet anyone who is interested at the bar for a cigar and brandy! Chef Joseph, thank you for a superb dinner!"

Joseph's playful frown evaporated and he gave Mr. Shmooze an enormous hug, whispering something to him as they embraced. With that, the movable feast retired to the lounge, where we were at once greeted by several familiar faces....

"Hey, Shmooze! Buddy! Over here!"

TO ORDER

Visit our website at www.mrshmooze.com

or call us at (877) MRSHMOOZE

(Call us regarding volume discounts for orders of 50 or more copies).